The Metaphors of Like

BrennerBooks

Published by Robert C. Brenner, 2025.

While every precaution has been taken in the preparation of this book, the publisher assumes no responsibility for errors or omissions, or for damages resulting from the use of the information contained herein.

THE METAPHORS OF LIKE

First edition. January 6, 2025.

Copyright © 2025 BrennerBooks.

ISBN: 978-1930199521

Written by BrennerBooks.

THE METAPHORS OF LIKE
Creating Mental Images with Words

by
Robert C. Brenner

ISBN 978-1-930199-52-1

©December 2024 All rights reserved. All contents and information herein are the sole property of the author. Reproduction, translation, or republishing of all or any part of this work is not authorized. Brief quotations of the material in this book may be used provided full prominent credit is given as follows: "From *The Metaphors of "Like"* by Robert C. Brenner." For larger excerpts or reprint rights, contact the publisher (brennerbooks@san.rr.com).

Notice: The book that you're holding is for your personal enjoyment only. A lot of hard work and substantial expense are behind its creation. If you would like to share this book with another person, please donate for an additional copy for each recipient. If you're reading this book and did not purchase it, or it was not purchased for your use only, please donate for your own copy. Thank you for respecting the hard work of this author and the financial investment that made this research notebook possible.

NOTICE: Fair Use Copyright Disclaimer

"Under Section 107 of the Copyright Act 1976, allowance is made for "fair use" for purposes such as criticism, comment, news reporting, teaching, scholarship, and research. Fair use is permitted by copyright statute that might otherwise be infringing. Non-profit, educational, research, or personal use tips the balance in favor of fair use."

Any use of copyrighted material is done for research, comment, or educational purposes. The publisher does not endorse any product, place, or person inferred by creators of copyrighted material presented herein for criticism, comment, research, or educational purposes under the Fair Use allowance quoted above.

CAUTION
DON'T PLAGIARIZE!

The writers who created the metaphors described in this book worked hard to give us great books. Each of these people deserves your respect and acknowledgement for their efforts. Don't insult them or our industry by copying their prose. Create your own words. Several authors have stolen author's metaphors exactly as they were written. This is wrong. These dishonest writers lost and are less for it because of their actions. But we are all affected by their poor decisions. Don't take others written work.

The books mentioned in this research report were studied in detail to understand why these works are so good. We provide these research results not so you could copy them, but so you can understand why these authors are the best in the business. Respect this. Respect them. Don't plagiarize.

INTRODUCTION

Websters's Collegiate Dictionary defines "metaphor" as *"The application of a word or phrase to an object or concept it does not literally denote, suggesting comparison to that object or concept."* The Oxford Dictionary says *it's a figure of speech that directly refers to one thing by mentioning another. It can provide clarity or identify hidden similarities between two different ideas.*

The creative use of words is a craft, and as writers mature in their craft, those who learn the best use of words find their works becoming ever more popular among readers or listeners who appreciate the mental images these words create.

You can recognize the better authors by their use of metaphors. By examining what they create, you too can create words that are more descriptive and interesting. Everyone wins when your words come alive in the minds of your audience or individual reader or listener.

The following are metaphors captured during our research. These authors are the most successful. Learn from them and you'll realize rewards you never dreamed possible (until now).

Here are the authors in order of the number of metaphors found in their writing:

John Steinbeck – *The Winter of Our Discontent* (66 entries)
Catherine Coulter – *Reckoning* (36 entries)
Jim Bishop – *The Day Christ Died* (33 entries)
Nora Roberts – *Jewels of the Sun* (32 entries)

John Steinbeck – *the Wayward Bus* (29 entries)
Tom Clancy – *Patriot Games* (26 entries)
Tom Clancy – *The Cardinal of the Kremlin* (25 entries)
Tom Clancy – *Red Storm Rising* (24 entries)
Bethany Campbell – *Heartland* (24 entries)
Robert Louis Stevenson – *Treasure Island* (20 entries)
Charlotte Lamb – *Circle of Fate* (20 entries)
J.D. Robb (- *Abandoned in Death* (16 entries)
Catherine Coulter – *Power Play* (16 entries)
C.S. Forrester – *The Captain from Connecticut* (15 entries)
Sally Stewart – *Love Upon the Wind* (13 entries)
John Steinbeck – *Of Mice and Men* (13 entries)
Robyn Donald - *Country of the Heart* 11 entries)
Nora Roberts – *Midnight Shadows* (11 entries)
Pearl S. Buck - *The Living Reed* (10 entries)
Alstair MacLean – *The Secret Ways* (10 entries)

Here are useful takeaways from studying the above list: First, the most descriptive authors are the quite successful. Second, other authors produced good content, but they only had one or few books published. Third, the very successful authors penned multiple books. Their skills matured as they wrote more. Perhaps these are helpful goals for you to adopt.

Here's what we scanned in our research:

ABANDONED IN DEATH by J. D. Robb
ADVENTURE ROAD magazine, Sep/Oct 1987
AGENT TO THE RESCUE by Lisa Childs
BEHOLD ISRAEL, Amir Tsarfati 23Apr2024
BRIT-AM 3319
CIRCLE OF FATE by Charlotte Lamb
Comment by Robert W. Malone MD, 29July2023
CONSERVATIVE UNDERGROUND NEWS Tucker Carlson comment 12January2024
COUNTRY OF THE HEART by Robyn Donald

DAILY NEWS ELECTION SPECIAL podcast June 16, 2024
DAN BONGINO PODCAST 20Dec2023
DESPERATION IN DEATH by J.D. Robb
DISCOVERING DANIEL by Amir Tsarfati
FEAR THE DARK by Kay Hooper
FINAL TARGET by Iris Johansen
FORTUNE DATA SHEET
HEARTLAND by Bethany Campbell
INSIGHT Article by Jane Addams Allen 23Nov1987
JEWELS OF THE SUN by Nora Roberts
KOINIONA HOUSE article by Ron Matsen
KUSI TV weather reporter 26Jan2024
KUSI TV weather reporter 31 August 2023
LEAGUE OF POWER 8Feb2024
LOVE UPON THE WIND by Sally Stewart
MIDNIGHT SHADOWS by Nora Roberts
NEWSMAX 21Apr2024
OPERATION JOKTAN by Amir Tsarfati and Steve Yohn
OUT TO CANAAN by Jan Karon
PATRIOT GAMES by Tom Clancy
Podcast by Dick Morris March 5, 2024
PORTALS OF PRAYER April – June 2024
POWER PLAY by Catherine Coulter
QUINN by Iris Johansen
QUORA comment by Robert Sheckley14Sep2023
RECKONING by Catherine Coulter
RED STORM RISING by Tom Clancy
RENEWED RIGHT.COM podcast 2Dec202
Sermon by Harry Majewski March 1, 2023
SOUTHWEST MAGAZINE, Oct 2018
SUNSET PASS by Zane Grey
SUCCESS, November 1987
TARZAN AT THE EARTH'S CORE by Edgar Rice Burroughs
THE 2019 OLD FARMER'S ALMANAC
THE BECOMING by Nora Roberts
THE CAPTAIN FROM CONNECTICUT by C.S. Forester
THE CARDINAL OF THE KREMLIN by Tom Clancy
THE CHRISTIAN SCIENE MONITOR article by Melvin Maddocks,
THE DAY CHRIST DIED by Jim Bishop

THE METAPHORS OF LIKE 7

THE FELLOWSHIP OF THE RING by J.R.R. Tolkien
THE GUNS OF NAVORONE by Alistair Maclean
THE HUNT FOR RED OCTOBER by Tom Clancy
THE IMPROBABILITY OF LOVE by Hannah Rothschild
THE LAST SECOND by Catherine Coulter
THE LIVING REED by Pearl S. Buck
THE MYSTERY OF THE SPIRAL BRIDGE by Franklin W. Dixon
THE NAVATAEANS – THE FINAL DAYS OF PETRA by Amir Tsarfati
THE NEW YORK SUN article by James Brooke on President Putin
THE OLD MAN AND THE SEA by Ernest Hemingway
THE RADIO BOYS AT MOUNTAIN PASS by Allen Chapman
THE RISE OF MAGICKS by Nora Roberts
THE SANDS OF TIME by Sidney Sheldon
THE SECRET WAYS by Alstair MacLean
THE SKY AND THE FOREST by C. S. Forester
THE WAYWARD BUS by John Steinbeck
TOWARD MORE PICTURESQUE SPEECH sidebar in Readers Digest
TREASURE ISLAND by Robert Louis Stevenson
UNDETECTED by Dee Henderson
VORTEX by Catherine Coulter
WALL STREET JOURNAL, 12November2021
WATCHING FOR THE WIND by James G. Edinger

Whether you're writing, speaking, or teaching, this book is for you. Here are 969 entries to prove my point about metaphors.

<back>

METAPHORS

ACT LIKE: ACTION: WALK: (PERSON) He had not walked half a block before he came to another saloon, the familiar look of which, and the barely decipherable name—Happy Days—acted like a blow in his face. (*SUNSET PASS* by Zane Grey)

ADOPT: LIKE DUCK TAKES TO WATER: (PERSON): He took to it like a duck takes to water. (*THE BECOMING* by Nora Roberts)

AFRAID: LIKE RESTAURANT: (PERSON) It scared the crap out of him waking up in the blistering heat and thinking about all the snakes and crawling critters eyeing him like a four-star restaurant. (*RECKONING* by Catherine Coulter)

AIR: LIKE SOFT KISS FROM EARTH: (PLACE) This avenue has a wideness that I love. It's open and reminds me of our walks in the park in the days when we were barely older than teens. I love the cracked sidewalk and the way the cats stalk about, the owners of all they survey. I don't care what the weather is, I carry an umbrella and my sweater is warm. My eyes eat up the green leaves above and the air is like a soft kiss from the earth. (Unknown)

ALCOHOL: LIKE ANY GOOD RUSSIAN: (THING) Like any good Russian, he felt that vodka was a much of life as air. (*THE CARDINAL OF THE KREMLIN* by Tom Clancy)

ALERT: LIKE LIZARD: (PERSON) ... seems to be able to look in all directions at once, like the lizards do in the outback. It was the only way to survive. (*RECKONING* by Catherine Coulter)

ANGER: LIKE CAT: (PERSON) Her mouth fell open and she looked at him as though she hadn't heard what he said. Then her rage became cold and murderous. Hitting him with both her fists and spitting like a cat, she kicked and shoved him. (*THE WAYWARD BUS* by John Steinbeck)

ANGER: LIKE KNOTTED FIST: ASHAMED: (PERSON) He felt ashamed about his anger. He had a hard knot in his stomach, one he got when things were not going well, a fist-like knot. (*THE WAYWARD BUS* by John Steinbeck)

ANIMAL-LIKE: SWAMP: (PLACE) animal-like (Unknown)

APPEAR: LIKE BLIGHT: (PLACE) I visited this place long before the tourists and fancy hotels/resorts appeared like blight on the landscape. (*THE NAVATAEANS – THE FINAL DAYS OF PETRA* by Amir Tsarfati)

APPEAR: LIKE DINOSAUR COMING TO PICNIC: (THING) Like a dinosaur coming to the picnic, a massive object appeared on the horizon, apparently coming overland at high speed. (*RED STORM RISING* by Tom Clancy)

APPEAR: LOOKED LIKE ENGLISH SHEEPDOG: (THING) he looked like an Old English sheepdog after a heavy night. (*CIRCLE OF FATE* by Charlotte Lamb)

APPEAR: LOOKED LIKE MOUNTAINS WERE DIPPED IN SUGAR: (THING) ... light snow and cold air made the mountains look like they were dipped in sugar. (*Unknown*)

APPEAR: LOOKED LIKE SCRUBBED TEENAGER: (THING) Without her makeup and tousled hair, she looked like a scrubbed teenager. (*RECKONING* by Catherine Coulter)

APPROVAL DROPPED: LIKE BOULDER: (PERSON) his approval dropped like a giant boulder off the side of a steep cliff. (*INTERNET*)

ARCH: LIKE SHOT PUT: EYEBROWS: (PERSON) his eyebrows arched like the trajectory of a soaring shot put. (The Hardy Boys Mystery Stories – THE MYSTERN OF THE SPIRAL BRIDGE by Franklin W. Dixon)

ARCHED: LIKE TRAJECTORY: (PERSON) His eyebrows arched like the trajectory of a soaring shot put. (*THE MYSTERN OF THE SPIRAL BRIDGE* by Franklin W. Dixon)

ARGUE OVER: LIKE DOGS: (PERSON) ... quarreling over ... like a pack of dogs over a bone. (*TARZAN AT THE EARTH'S CORE* by Edgar Rice Burroughs)

ARGUE: LIKE TAUNTING BULL IN FIELD: (PERSON) arguing with a man with a temper is like crossing an open field and taunting a bull nearby. (*CIRCLE OF FATE* by Charlotte Lamb)

ARM CAST STICKING OUT: LIKE CLAW: (PERSON) The cast on his arm was so heavy that it ruined his balance. He stood a little too fast and nearly smashed into the car next to him, but he caught himself with an angry shake of the head before anyone had to grab for him. He stood still for a moment, his left arm sticking out like the big claw on a fiddler crab. (*PATRIOT GAMES* by Tom Clancy)

ARMED GUARDS: LIKE COMMANDOS: (THING) I was halfheartedly arranging muskmelons in the doorway stands when the old-fashioned green armored car pulled up in front of the bank. Two guards armed like commandos got out of the back and carried gray sacks of money into the bank. In about ten minutes they came out and got into the riveted fortress and it drove away. (*THE WINTER OF OUR DISCONTENT* by John Steinbeck)

ASSOCIATE WITH OTHERS: LIKE HIMSELF: (PERSON) He was a businessman, president of a medium-sized corporation, and he was never alone. His business was conducted by groups of men who worked alike, thought alike, and even looked alike. His lunches were with men like himself who joined together in clubs so that no foreign element or idea could enter. His religious life was again his lodge and his church, both of which were screened and protected. One night a week he played poker with men so exactly like himself that the game was fairly even, and from this fact his group was convinced that they were very fine poker players. Wherever he went he was not one man but a unit in a corporation, a unit in a club, in a lodge, in a church, in a political party. His thoughts and ideas were never subjected to criticism since he willingly associated only with people like himself. He read a newspaper written by and for his group. He books that came into his house were chosen by a committee which deleted material that might irritate him. He hated foreign countries and foreigners because it was difficult to find his counterpart in them. He did not want to stand out from his group. He would like to have risen to the top of it and be admired by it, but it would not occur to him to leave it. (*THE WAYWARD BUS* by John Steinbeck)

ATTACK: LIKE TIGER: (PERSON) She wheeled upon him like a young tiger. (*TARZAN AT THE EARTH'S CORE* by Edgar Rice Burroughs)

ATTITUDE: LIKE SAND TRAP: (PERSON) Failure is a state of mind. It's like one of those sand traps an ant lion digs. You keep sliding back. It takes a hell of a jump to get out of it. Once you get out, you find success is a state of mind too. (*THE WINTER OF OUR DISCONTENT* by John Steinbeck)

ATTITUDE: LIKE PEOPLE: (PERSON) [Like] people who have a firm repulsion to anything [fill in the blank] they eat this stuff up, and arrogantly spread lies and untruths around like mucus on a baby's bib. (comment posted online)

ATTITUDE: LIKE PEOPLE: (PERSON) Like most modern people, I don't believe in prophecy or magic and then spend half my time practicing it. (*THE WINTER OF OUR DISCONTENT* by John Steinbeck)

ATTITUDE: LIKE SYRUP: PERSON:... a demeanor like syrup that wouldn't pour. (Readers Digest *TOWARD MORE PICTURESQUE SPEECH*)

ATTRACT: LIKE MAGIC SPELL: (THING) he scent of bacon and eggs drew her on like a magic spell. (*HEARTLAND* by Bethany Campbell)

AVOID: LIKE PLAGUE: (PERSON) After that she avoided him like the plague. (*LOVE UPON THE WIND* by Sally Stewart)

AWAKEN: LIKE MORNING YAWN: (THING) March winds, like a morning yawn, awaken the land to spring (Unknown)

BACK OFF: LIKE CAT ON HOT COALS: (PERSON) She backed off like a cat on hot coals. (*QUINN* by Iris Johansen)

BACK OFF: LIKE CAT ON HOT TIN ROOF: (PERSON) backed off like a cat on a hot tin roof. (*Author*)

BEACH SCENE: LIKE DREAM: (PLACE) dreamlike

BECAME: LIKE WAX: (PERSON) At the first sign of trouble they became like wax in his hands. (Unknown)

BEHAVING: LIKE HORSE: She was behaving like a horse in the hands of incompetent stable boys. (*THE CAPTAIN FROM CONNECTICUT* by C.S. Forester)

BEND DOWN: LIKE PENITENT: CROPS: (PLACE) And the crops changed. Fruit trees took the place of grain fields, and vegetables to feed the world spread out on the bottoms; lettuce, cauliflower, artichokes, potatoes—stoop crops. A man may stand to use a scythe, a plow, a pitchfork; but he must crawl like a bug between the rows of lettuce, he must bend his back and pull his long bag between the cotton rows, he must go on his knees like a penitent across a cauliflower patch (*THE GRAPES OF WRATH* by John Steinbeck)

BEND: LIKE CELLOPHANE: BOMB HOLE: (THING) His mind kept coming back to the image of the four-inch-thick flight deck steel bent into the sky like cellophane, a blackened cavern below it where the hangar deck used to be. (*RED STORM RISING* by Tom Clancy)

BENT OVER: LIKE OLD MAN: (PERSON) He was a poor specimen of man. His face was gashed and raw and swollen so that purple welts marked his cheekbones, and both eyes were puffed. His hands shook in the fetters and he was bent over like a person of twice his years. (*THE DAY CHRIST DIED* by Jim Bishop)

BENT: LIKE WILLOW: MAN: (PERSON) Unlike a sturdy oak, he bent like a willow in the wind. (*Unknown*)

BENT: SLAB-LIKE: AIRCRAFT: (THING) Nearly all tactical aircraft had pleasing lines conferred on them by the need in combat for speed and maneuverability. Not the Hog, which was perhaps the ugliest bird ever built for the U.S. Air Force. Her twin turbofan engines hung like afterthoughts at the twin-rudder tail, itself a throwback to the thirties. Her slab-like wings had not a whit of sweepback and were bent in the middle to accommodate the clumsy landing gear. The undersides of the wings were studded with many hard points so ordnance could be carried, and the fuselage was built around the aircraft's primary weapon, the GAU-8 thirty-millimeter rotary cannon designed specifically to smash Soviet tanks. *(THE HUNT FOR RED OCTOBE by* Tom Clancy*)*

BIRDS BLOWN ABOUT: LIKE RAGS: (THING) ... spring dodged back toward winter with cold rain and raw gusty wind that shredded the tender leaves of too trusting trees. The bold and concupiscent bull sparrows on the lawns, intent on lechery, got blown about like rags, off course and off target, and they chattered wrathfully against the inconstant weather. The tail of one familiar bird got blown sideways like a battle flag. *(THE WINTER OF OUR DISCONTENT* by John *Steinbeck)*

BIRDS TAIL BLOWN SIDEWAYS: LIKE BATTLE FLAG: (THING) ... spring dodged back toward winter with cold rain and raw gusty wind that shredded the tender leaves of too trusting trees. The bold and concupiscent bull sparrows on the lawns, intent on lechery, got blown about like rags, off course and off target, and they chattered wrathfully against the inconstant weather. The tail of one familiar bird got blown sideways like a battle flag. *(THE WINTER OF OUR DISCONTENT* by John *Steinbeck)*

BIRTH ASPECTS: LIKE TWO-COLOR GARMENT: (PERSON) The natural and supernatural aspects of this birth were so thoroughly integrated that, like a two-color garment, it was impossible to pull the thread of one for examination without destroying the raiment. (*MIDNIGHT SHADOWS* by Nora Roberts)

BLAME: LIKE TWO BALD MEN FIGHTING OVER A COMB: (PERSON) Trying to blame each other is like two bald men fighting over a comb. (*BIBLE* 2 Samuel 2:1-3, 39)

BLEED OUT: LIKE WATER: (PERSON) Blood pumped out like water from a hose. (*STRANGERS* by Dean R. Koontz)

BLOOM: ACTION: HOPE: (PERSON) Harry felt hope bloom like the crocuses his mother had planted when he'd been a little boy. (*NIGHTWORK* by Nora Roberts)

BLOOMED BITTER: LIKE BRUISE: (THING) The few lights that worked cast purple shadows along with sickly yellow glows so the pools and splashes of them bloomed bitter, like a bruise. (*DEVOTED IN DEATH by J.D.Robb*)

BLOSSOMS: LIKE WHITE WATERS IN SHALLOW SEA: VALLEY: (PLACE) The spring is beautiful in California valleys in which the fruit blossoms are fragrant pink and white (like) waters in a shallow sea. (*THE GRAPES OF WRATH* by John Steinbeck)

BLOW THROUGH: ACTION: WATCH: (PERSON) Harry stood back, watched his mother rearrange her letters, and felt the love for both of them blow through him like a warm wind. (*NIGHTWORK* by Nora Roberts)

BLOWBACK: LIKE PEEING INTO WIND: (PERSON) like peeing into the wind. (Author)

BLOWS: LIKE SLEDGE HAMMER: (THING) A police officer with a Maglite stood over the remains of the Harley motorcycle. Something like a sledge hammer was used to make repeated blows on the machine. There was rage in those blows. (*POWER PLAY* by Catherine Coulter)

BLUE MOONLIGHT: LIKE GIANT FLASHLIGHT: (THING) The blue moon was like a giant flashlight in the eyes. (*KUSI TV* weather reporter 31 August 2023)

BOTTOM SPREADING: LIKE RIPE BRIE: (PERSON) her bottom spread over the sofa like ripe Brie. *(THE IMPROBABILITY OF LOVE by Hannah Rothschild)*

BOW HEAD: LIKE BULLRUSH: (PERSON) ... to bow down his head like a bulrush. (*THE HOLY BIBLE* Isaiah 58:3-11)

BOWLS OF FLOWERS: LIKE BEING IN FLOWER SHOP: (PERSON) She kept great bowls of flowers in her house always, so that her friends said it was like being in a florist's shop and she arranged them herself so beautifully. (THE WAYWARD BUS by John Steinbeck)

BREATH CONDENSATION EVAPORATING: LIKE SMOKE IN STILL FROZEN AIR: COLD: ... bitterly cold ... The icy air turned chins and ears and nose tips red and blue and white, and the condensation of breath was heavy and almost like smoke, evaporating slowly like smoke in the still, frozen air. *(THE SECRET WAYS* by Alistair MacLean)

BREATH HUNG: LIKE SMOKE: (PERSON) His breath hung like smoke in his wake as he strode off. (*TREASURE ISLAND* by Robert Louis Stevenson)

BREATHE: LIKE INHALING KNIVES: (PERSON) Breathing the cold air off the river was like inhaling knives. His nose and mouth were like sandpaper and his heart threatened to burst from his chest. He hadn't jogged in months, and he was paying the price for his sloth. (*PATRIOT GAMES* by Tom Clancy)

BREATHE: LIKE SANDPAPER KNIVES: (PERSON) Breathing the cold air off the river was like inhaling knives. His nose and mouth were like sandpaper and his heart threatened to burst from his chest. He hadn't jogged in months, and he was paying the price for his sloth. (*PATRIOT GAMES* by Tom Clancy)

BREATHE: LIKE STICKING HEAD OUT CAR WINDOW: (PERSON) The experience is a little like sticking your head out a car window at highway speed. The wind blows so hard you forget to breathe. (*SUCCESS*, November 1987)

BREEZE: LIKE CARESS: (PERSON) He strolled along the shore dressed in a light windbreaker, sweatpants, and sneakers, staying just above the tide line, salt-tinged semitropical breezes slipping over his cheeks like a warm caress. (*POWER PLAYS POLITIKA* by Tom Clancy and Martin Greenberg)

BROKE SURFACE: LIKE BROACHING WHALE: (THING) The [submarine] soared up through the surface of the Atlantic like a broaching whale, coming three quarters of her length out of the water before crashing back. (*THE HUNT FOR RED OCTOBER* by Tom Clancy)

BROWS: LIKE FINGERNAILS: TURTLE: THING:... over the grass at the roadside a land turtle crawled, turning aside for nothing, dragging his high-domed shell over the grass. His hard legs and yellow-nailed feet threshed slowly through the grass, not really walking, but boosting and dragging his shell along. The barley beads slid off his shell, and the clover burrs fell on him and rolled to the ground. His horny beak was partly open, and his fierce, humorous eyes, under brows like fingernails, stared straight ahead. He came over the grass leaving a beaten trail behind him, and the hill, which was the highway embankment, reared up ahead of him. For a moment he stopped, his head held high. He blinked and looked up and down. At last he started to climb the embankment. Front clawed feet reached forward but did not touch. The hind feet kicked his shell along, and it scraped on the grass, and on the gravel. As the embankment grew steeper and steeper, the more frantic were the efforts of the land turtle. Pushing hind legs strained and slipped, boosting the shell along, and the horny head protruded as far as the neck could stretch. Little by little the shell slid up the embankment until at last a parapet cut straight across its line of march, the shoulder of the road, a concrete wall four inches high. As though they worked independently the hind legs pushed the shell against the wall. The head upraised and peered over the wall to the broad smooth plain of cement. Now the hands raced on top of the wall, strained and lifted, and the shell came slowly up and rested its front end on the wall. For a moment the turtle rested. A red ant ran into the shell, into the soft skin inside the shell, and suddenly head and legs snapped in, and the armored tail clamped in sideways. The red ant was crushed between body and legs. And one head of wild oats was clamped into the shell by a front leg. For a long moment the turtle lay still, and then the neck crept out and the old humorous frowning eyes looked about and the legs and tail came out. The back legs went to work, straining like elephant legs, and the shell tipped to an angle so that the front legs could not reach the level cement plain. But higher and higher the hind legs boosted it, until at last the center of balance was reached, the front tipped down, the front legs scratched at the pavement, and it was up. But the head of wild oats was held by its stem around the front legs. - Now the going was easy, and all the legs worked, and the shell boosted along, waggling from side to side. ... now it hurried on, for the highway was burning hot. A light truck approached, and as it came near, the driver saw the turtle and swerved to hit it. His front wheel struck the edge of the shell, flipped the turtle like a tidily-wink, spun it like a coin, and rolled it off the highway. The truck went back to its course along the right side. Lying on its back, the turtle was tight in its shell for a long time. But at last its legs waved in the air, reaching for something to pull it over. Its front foot caught a piece of quartz and little by little the shell pulled over and flopped upright. The wild oat head fell out and three of the spearhead seeds stuck in the ground. And as the turtle crawled on down the embankment, its shell dragged dirt over the seeds. The turtle entered a dirt road and jerked itself along, drawing a wavy shallow trench in the dust with its shell. The old humorous eyes looked ahead, and the horny beak opened a little. His yellow toe nails slipped a fraction in the dust. *(THE GRAPES OF WRATH* by John Steinbeck)

BRUISE: LIKE AUSTRALIA: (PERSON) She stood naked in front of her bathroom mirror, staring at the bright purple bruises on her arms, her shoulders, and her chest. She looked over her shoulder, and saw her back looked like a multicolor flag and the bruise on her butt something like Australia. The face in the mirror staring back at her looked like oatmeal. (*VORTEX* by Catherine Coulter)

BRUSH OF DEATH: LIKE NAKED WOMAN'S TOUCH: (THING) ... felt the emptiness, the waves of death brushing against me, like a naked woman's touch. (REDDIT WRITER'S GROUP posting)

BUGGED OUT EYES: LIKE BLIND: (PERSON) His lungs burned and cried for air, but he did not stop running. He went through the wealthy residential section of the city, little legs flying, eyes bugged like those of one who does not see, and to those out for a morning stroll he was a comical figure. (*THE DAY CHRIST DIED* by Jim Bishop)

BUILT: LIKE BRAWLER: (PERSON) He had the rawboned face of the Celts, with the wild good looks that the fine genes of his parents had blended, with a long, straight nose, a mouth full and shamelessly sensual, a tough, take-a-punch chin with just a hint of a cleft. He was built like a brawler—wide of shoulder, long of arm, and narrow of hip. And indeed, he had spent a good portion of his youth planting his fists in faces or taking them in his own. As much, he wasn't ashamed to admit, for the fun of it as for temper. (*JEWELS OF THE SUN* by Nora Roberts)

BUILT: LIKE LINEBACKER: (PERSON) He was built like a linebacker with shoulders wide as a redwood; he had a shaved head and soft, worried blue eyes. He wore a pale gray suit with an open-collar white shirt, and stuck out a hand that gripped—and swallowed—hers. (ABANDONED IN DEATH by J. D. Robb)

BUNDLE UP: ACTION: RIDE: (PERSON) He took the train, just a teenage boy bundled up to the eyeballs like everyone else on a gusty, snowy night in Chicago. (*NIGHTWORK* by Nora Roberts)

BUNK: LIKE BEING IN COFFIN: (THING) The bunk on the submarine was always the same—hard against the curved hull of the submarine. It was like being in a coffin with the lid half-open. (*THE CARDINAL OF THE KREMLIN* by Tom Clancy)

BURL: LIKE TICK: (THING) burled under his skin like a tick. (Unknown)

BURN: LIKE ACID: (PERSON) She wept tears so bitter they burned into her soul like acid. (*THE BECOMING* by Nora Roberts)

CALM DAY: LIKE THIS: RIVER: (PLACE) The surface of the river was never still; a storm would work it up into great rollers, and on a calm day like this, when at first sight the surface seemed almost oily, closer observation would reveal great swirls and motiveless crinklings, sinister, ugly movements as the broad water went sliding along, coming from nowhere, going nowhere, hateful and fearsome in its majesty. (*THE SKY AND THE FOREST* by C. S. Forester)

Campbell)

CANNON SOUND: LIKE ENORMOUS ZIPPER: (THING) The portside mount fired first, the six-barrel cannon making a sound like that of an enormous zipper. Its radar system tracked the target, and tracked the outgoing slugs ... (*RED STORM RISING* by Tom Clancy)

CARRY: LIKE RED FURRY COLLAR: (PERSON) They carried dead sacrificial lambs across the backs of their necks, like red furry collars. Some carried them slung by the legs. (*THE DAY CHRIST DIED* by Jim Bishop)

CENTERED: LIKE WHITE OVAL IN GUNSIGHT: SATELLITE: (THING) The range readout was rapidly dropping as the satellite came toward them, circling its way around the earth at 18,000 miles an hour. The image the engineers saw was of a slightly oblong blob, white with internal heat against a sky devoid of warmth. It was exactly in the center of the targeting reticle, like a white oval in a gunsight. (*THE CARDINAL OF THE KREMLIN* by Tom Clancy)

CHANGE: LIKE UNDERWEAR: (PERSON) He wanted to walk away and disappear. He wanted to take off his old life like a suit of underwear. (*THE DAY CHRIST WAS BORN* by Jim Bishop)

CHANGE: LIKE HURLING BOWLING BALL: (THING) Change came like a bowling ball hurling toward a porcelain pin. It struck with pulverizing force leaving behind a fine dust that was carried away by the breeze eventually settling over all of our lives. (*DISCOVERING DANIEL* by Amir Tsafarti)

CHANGE: LIKE LOOKING: (PERSON) ... proved to me that some deep-down underwater change was going on in me. It's like looking at wall-paper samples and I had just unrolled a new pattern. (*THE WINTER OF OUR DISCONTENT* by John Steinbeck)

CHANGING LANDSCAPE: LIKE JUNGLE: ZOO: (PLACE) The San Diego Zoo's witty and erudite bus drivers/guides provide a running commentary as they took visitors through a rapidly changing landscape, from jungle-like terrain punctuated by bird cries to a series of sloping hills dotted with rare deer, antelope and mountain goats. (*ADVENTURE ROAD* magazine Sep-Oct 1987)

CHARACTERS: LOOKED LIKE ZOMBIES: (THING) these characters looked like zombies. (*HEARTLAND* by Bethany Campbell)

CLEAVE WATER: LIKE FURRY WHISPERS: OTTERS: (PLACE) In the reedy edges of the inner waters, the mallards nested and brought out their young flotillas, muskrats dug communities and swam lithely in the early morning. The ospreys hung, aimed, and plummeted on fish, and sea gulls carried clams and scallops high in the air and dropped them to break them open for eating. Some otters still clove the water like secret furry whispers; rabbits poached in the gardens and gray squirrels moved like little waves in the streets of the village. Cock pheasants flapped and coughed their crowing. Blue herons poised in the shallow water like leggy rapiers and at night the bitterns cried out like lonesome ghosts. *(THE WINTER OF OUR DISCONTENT by John Steinbeck)*

CLING: LIKE BODY SPRAY: (PERSON) His eyes told her he'd recently inhaled some drug, the smoke from which still clung to his clothes like a sickly-sweet body spray. (*ABANDONED IN DEATH* by J. D. Robb)

CLOSING DOOR AFTER DOOR: LIKE TRAP NEST: (PERSON) He had walked through closing door after closing door in the maze. It was rather like a trap nest. A hen finds a hole, looks in, sees there is a bit of grain, steps through the door—the door closes. Well here is a nest. It's dark and quiet. Why not lay an egg? It'd be a good joke on whoever left that door open.

CLOUDS ROLL IN: LIKE DUMPLINGS: (THING) Light was creeping up the sky and over the mountains. The colorless dawn of greys and blacks moved in so that white and blue things were silver and red and dark green things were black. The new leaves on the big oaks were black and white, and the mountain rims were sharp. Lumpish, heavy clouds that rolled in the sky like dumplings were beginning to take on a faint rose-pink color on their eastern edges. (*THE WAYWARD BUS* by John Steinbeck)

CLOUDS: LOOKED LIKE SNOW MOUNTAINS: COASTLINE: (PLACE) He could not see the green of the shore now but only the tops of the blue hills that showed white as though they were snow-capped and the clouds that looked like high snow mountains above them. The sea was very dark and the light made prisms in the water. (*THE OLD MAN AND THE SEA* by Ernest Hemingway)

CLOUDS: LOOKED LIKE WHIPPED CREAM: (THING) When it rained, it did so at night, and the days were golden and sweet-smelling, the essence of every connotation that the word "summer" can inspire. Days when the sky was a deep, burning blue and the clouds like whipped cream, days of heat so tangible that it could almost be touched, days spent carefully sunbathing to toast her slender paleness into gold. (*COUNTRY OF THE HEART* by Robyn Donald)

CLUNKY-LOOKING: MOTEL ROOM: (PLACE) His room, he saw when he carted his duffel and backpack inside, boasted a single bed covered with a green-and-blue-floral spread, a single dresser on which sat a clunky-looking TV, a green carpet, beige walls. He had lamps on stands on either side of the bed and a tiny bathroom, which, to his very experienced eye, actually looked more than acceptably clean.. (*NIGHTWORK* by Nora Roberts)

COBWEBS: LIKE EARLY HOLLYWEEN: BASEMENT: (PLACE) The basement looked like something from a 1940s movie set. There were thick cobwebs everywhere, like Halloween had come early. (*RECKONING* by Catherine Coulter)

COFFEE SMELL: LIKE FRESH PERKED COFFEE: (THING) ... smelled like freshly-perked coffee. (*Unknown*)

COLD WIND: STRUCK LIKE KNIFE: (THING) It was so cold outside that his windows were still heavily frosted, and he had to open them to see what the weather was like. The wind was light, but it struck through his thin shirt like a knife, and it had all the makings of an ideal night for an agent *(THE SECRET WAYS* by Alstair MacLean*)*

COLLAPSE: LIKE BALLOON: (PERSON) pride and everything else collapsed, like a pricked balloon. (*BEYOND HER CONTROL* by Jessica Steele)

COLOR OF MOSS: KELP-LIKE: FOREST: (PLACE) Upon the forest floor lie trees of yesteryear, fallen in storms long forgotten. The seasons have been harsh, stripping away the bark and outer layers, yet rendering them all the more beautiful. They have the appearance of driftwood, twisting in patterns that remind Sarah of seaside waves; even the color of the moss is kelp-like. They are soft, damp, yet her fingers come away dry. Sarah tilts her head upward, feeling her hair tumble further down her back; the pines are several houses tall, reaching toward the golden rays of spring. Birdsong comes in lulls and bursts, the silence and the singing working together as well as any improvised melody. A new smile paints itself upon her freckled face, rose-pink lips semi-illuminated by the dappled light. Before she knows it her feet have begun to walk body and mind both on autopilot - it's morning-time and no-one expects her home until supper. (Unknown)

COLOR: LOOKED LIKE TOP OF ROSY WAVE: (THING) The spirited color in her abstracted forms looked like the top of a surging rosy wave. (*INSIGHT* Article by Jane Addams Allen)

COLORFUL: LIKE KALEIDOSCOPE: RIDE: (PERSON) The rider slowed as they wound through woods, under trees where leaves tumbled down as the air shook them free. Still so much color remained it was like riding within a kaleidoscope with the sun sparkling through. (*THE BECOMING* by Nora Roberts)

COME OFF BOTTOM: LIKE SPAWNING SALMON: (THING) If the charges miss, he'll come off the bottom like a salmon at spawning time. (*RED STORM RISING* by Tom Clancy)

COMING LIKE NEW AND BETTER: (THING) Hope feels like spring, like something new and better is on the horizon. (*DISCOVERING DANIEL* by Amir Tsarfati)

COMPACT: LIKE THATCH: WOODS: (PLACE) He came to a long thicket of oak-like trees—live, or evergreen oaks. I heard afterward they should be called—which grew along the sand like brambles, the boughs curiously twisted, the foliage compact, like thatch. The thicket stretched down from the top of one of the sandy knolls, spreading and growing taller as it went, until it reached the margin of the broad, reedy fen, through which the nearest of the little rivers soaked its way into the anchorage. The marsh was steaming in the strong sun, and the outline of the Spyglass trembled through the haze. (*TREASURE ISLAND* by Robert Louis Stevenson)

COMPLAIN: LIKE WOMAN: PERSON:... acted like a woman going through life consistently demanding to see the manager. (*PATRIOT GAMES* by Tom Clancy)

COMPLEXION: LIKE CORPSE: (PERSON) His once-clear blue eyes were bloodshot and lifeless, the ruddy complexion gray like a corpse. His skin sagged, and the gray stubble on his cheeks blurred a face that had once been called handsome. (THE CARDINAL OF THE KREMLIN by Tom Clancy)

COMPLICATE: LIKE DRAWING SNAKE WITH LEGS: **(THING)** Like drawing a snake and adding feet unnecessarily complicating things. *(TOWARD MORE PICTURESQUE SPEECH)*

CONCRETE WALLS: LIKE VILLA: STREET: (PLACE) The street was glorious in its inception. The sidewalks were smooth grey stones, joined with such precision that the joins were almost invisible. The walls were concrete, but not like a villa in rural Spain; they were more akin to the construction of a modernist skyscraper, all sharp edges and corners. The buildings were nothing short of monoliths, the bastions of the city's pride, stamping its arrival on the map of financially significant places to trade with. Yet no-one had communicated this vision to the citizenry. The street that should have been such a joy to walk was littered with garbage and the detritus of dogs. Enjoying the street view would mean taking your eye off your shoes, and no-one was about to do that. (Unknown)

CONTEST EVERY LUUMP: LIKE WOLVES DEFENDING CUBS: (PERSON) The Germans contested every lump of dirt in their country like wolves defending their cubs, retreating only when they were forced to, counterattacking at every opportunity, draining the blood from the advancing enemy units as they brought every weapon they had to bear. (*RED STORM RISING* by Tom Clancy)

CORDITE AND LIME SMELL: LIKE AFTERSHAVE: (THING) He smelled like cordite and lime, like the aftershave his father used to use. (*POWER PLAY* by Catherine Coulter)

COUGH: LIKE WILL-DE-BEAST: (PERSON) ... coughed like a will-de-beast. (Mike Adams situational podcast)

COUNTER GOLD FLECKS: LIKE BEACH SAND: KITCHEN: (PLACE) A serious sort of kitchen, with a massive cooktop and oven in addition to double Auto Chefs, miles of counter done in pale gold with tiny glinting flecks—like beach sand. A lot of serious kitchen tools in drawers, precisely organized. *(DEVOTED IN DEATH by J.D. Robb)*

COVER UP: LIKE BLANKET: (PERSON) ... covered like a blanket on a cold morning. (Author)

COVER: LIKE BLANKET: (PERSON) She remembered walking through the woods, surrounded by trees, with the sun pushing through the thick canopy of leaves and covering her like a blanket soaked in hot water. (*ABANDONED IN DEATH* by J. D. Robb)

COVER: LIKE DIRTY SNOW: (THING) Dust lay over every surface like dirty snow, pristine dust layer, not a foot print anywhere, papers and letters addressed to no one were piled up to the letter box and cascaded all the way to the foot of the rough wooden stairs, old tea cups lay on a coffee table thickly encrusted with dried up mold, dust covered mirrors, smell of mildew, stale air, air thick with dust, shafts of light bursting through gaps in the boarded up window, light streaming through the gaps in the heavy velvet curtains, absolute silence, the house's only occupants weaved their webs between the spindles of the stair banisters and from the ceiling to the wall, old cobwebs billowed in the draft. (Unknown)

COZY (PLACE) LIKED BEST: (PLACE) t was just the kind of place she liked best—cozy and candlelit, welcoming and yet discrete; where taste and service were all important but no one pressed their unwanted attentions on you. (Unknown)

CRACKLING SOUND: LIKE PISTOL SHOTS: (THING) The unexpected noise was the crackling of the frozen canvas as it was unrolled. And the frozen ropes crackled, too, like a whole succession of pistol shots, as they ran through the sheaves. Little lumps of ice stripped from them came raining down. (*THE CAPTAIN FROM CONNECTICUT* by C.S. Forester)

CRAWL: LIKE BUG: CROPS: (PLACE) And the crops changed. Fruit trees took the place of grain fields, and vegetables to feed the world spread out on the bottoms; lettuce, cauliflower, artichokes, potatoes—stoop crops. A man may stand to use a scythe, a plow, a pitchfork; but he must crawl like a bug between the rows of lettuce, he must bend his back and pull his long bag between the cotton rows, he must go on his knees like a penitent across a cauliflower patch *(THE GRAPES OF WRATH by John Steinbeck)*

CRAWL: LIKE BUG: HIGHWAY: (PLACE) Along the highway the cars of the migrant people crawled out like bugs, and the narrow concrete miles stretched ahead. *(THE GRAPES OF WRATH by John Steinbeck)*

CREAKING SOUND: LIKE SHIP IN HEAVY SEAWAY: (THING) The ancient train rocked and swayed alarmingly along the ill-maintained track, shuddering and straining whenever a snow-laden gust of wind from the southeast caught it broadside along its entire length and threatened for a heart-stopping moment, which was only one of a never-ending series of such moments, to topple it off the track. The carriage wheels, transmitting a teeth-rattling vibration through a suspension that had long since given up on an unequal battle with the years, screeched and grated in a shrilly metallic cacophony as they jarred and leapt across the uneven intersection of the rails. The wind and the snow whistled icily through a hundred cracks in ill-made doors and windows, the wooden coachwork and seats creaked and protested like a ship working in a heavy seaway, but the ancient train battered on steadily through the white blindness of the late afternoon in midwinter, sometimes slowing down unexpectedly on a straight stretch of track, at other times increasing speed unexpectedly round seemingly dangerous curves: the driver, one hand almost constantly on the steam whistle that whispered and died to a muffled extinction only a hundred yards away in the driving snow, was obviously a man with complete confidence in himself, the capacities of his train, and his knowledge of the track ahead. *(THE SECRET WAYS by Alstair MacLean)*

THE METAPHORS OF LIKE 27

CREAKING VOICE: LIKE HINGES OF RUSTY GATE: (THING) ... voice creaked like the hinges of a rusty iron gate. (*Readers Digest TOWARD MORE PICTURESQUE SPEECH*)

CREATE: LIKE DISNEY: (THING) a content factory like Disney. (*NEWSMAX* 21Apr2024)

CREEP: BEETLE-LIKE: (PERSON) He could see no sign of war in the drowsy town; the only things moving were his men's gigs, creeping beetle-like over the blue water toward the beach. It would be a long, dreary wait. (*THE CAPTAIN FROM CONNECTICUT* by C.S. Forester)

CREEP: LIKE BLACK SLUDGE: (PERSON) The darkness was going to swallow her up, she felt it, and watched helplessly as it swallowed up the others one by one, creeping up to them, over them, like some hideous black sludge, moving in terrifying slow motion, until ... (*FEAR THE DARK* by Kay Hooper)

CREEP: LIKE TIDE: (THING) The little farmers watched debt creep up on them like the tide. *(THE GRAPES OF WRATH* by John Steinbeck*)*

CREEP: SWAMP-LIKE VEGETATION: RIVER: (PLACE) In the heart of the forest, an idle river carried all the debris that fell in from above slowly downstream. Large boughs sprouted from the trees and reached into the murky water as if trying to scoop up the swarming fish. Although the warm water was an olive color from the swirling mud and algae, you could see the underwater wildlife flourish in the shallow part. Swamp-like vegetation and old, rotting trees crept into the river's edge and created slimy pools of debris from withered leaves, twigs and lemma. Above the mass of water, high branches wove a tunnel of green leaves like archways in a church to protect from strong sunlight. (Unknown)

CROWD BUNCHED: LIKE BANANAS: (PERSON) thousands of fans circled, most bunched like bananas (Online newsletter, *THE HILL*)

CROWD IN: LIKE ANTS: (PERSON) Pilgrims crowded in and out of the Fountain Gate like gray ants moving in and out of a hill. (*THE DAY CHRIST DIED* by Jim Bishop)

CRUMBLE: LIKE BRICKS OF DUST: (THING) While the dying world reeled, its framework—governments, technology, laws, transportations, communication—crumbled like bricks of dust. *(THE RISE OF MAGICKS* by Nora Roberts*)*

CRUMBLE: LIKE BUNCH OF BROCCOLI: (PERSON) She knocked him out with a kick to his side. He crumbled like a bunch of broccoli. (*OPERATION JOKTAN* by Amir Tsarfati and Steve Yohn)

CRUMBLE: LIKE SAND CASTLE: (PERSON) Barriers...began to crumble like sand castles under the assault of a high tide. (Unknown)

CRY OUT: LIKE LONESOME GHOSTS: MARSH: (PLACE) In the reedy edges of the inner waters, the mallards nested and brought out their young flotillas, muskrats dug communities and swam lithely in the early morning. The ospreys hung, aimed, and plummeted on fish, and sea gulls carried clams and scallops high in the air and dropped them to break them open for eating. Some otters still clove the water like secret furry whispers; rabbits poached in the gardens and gray squirrels moved like little waves in the streets of the village. Cock pheasants flapped and coughed their crowing. Blue herons poised in the shallow water like leggy rapiers and at night the bitterns cried out like lonesome ghosts. (*THE WINTER OF OUR DISCONTENT* by John Steinbeck)

CRY: LIKE BAGPIPES: (THING) A harmonica is easy to carry. Take it out of your hip pocket; knock it against your palm to shake out the dirt and pocket fuzz and bits of tobacco. Now it's ready. You can do anything with a harmonica, thin reedy single tone, or chords, or melody with rhythm chords. You can mold the music with curved hands, making it wail and cry like bagpipes, making it full and round like an organ, making it as sharp and bitter as the reed pipes of the hills.

And you can play and put it back in your pocket. It is always with you, always in your pocket. And as you play, you learn new tricks, new ways to mold the tone with your hands, to pinch the tone with your lips, and no one teaches you. Your foot taps gently on the ground. Your eyebrows rise and fall in rhythm. (*THE GRAPES OF WRATH* by John Steinbeck)

CRY: LIKE CHILD: (PERSON) She lay a long time on her back with her arms crossed over her face. Her sobbing stopped gradually, like a child's. The inside of her arm was warm and wet over her eyes. She was flooded with a kind of comfort, and the release from tension was as though a tight mesh had been loosed from her body. (*THE WAYWARD BUS* by John Steinbeck)

CRY: LIKE SPOILED CHILD: (PERSON) She wailed like a spoiled child. (*CIRCLE OF FATE* by Charlotte Lamb)

CRYING: LIKE A BABY: (PERSON) Not figuring the perp for a rabbit, the detective took him down and got a hole in the knee of her trousers for the effort. The perp was flopping around like a landed trout, and crying like a baby. (*MIDNIGHT SHADOWS* by Nora Roberts)

CURLED: LIKE SHRIMP: (PERSON) The man collapsed in a heap, curled up like a shrimp. (*MIDNIGHT SHADOWS* by Nora Roberts)

CURVED FINGER: LIKE HALF A TUBE: (PERSON) He tapped the counter with his fingers. He had let the little fingernail on his left hand grow very long. It was curved, like half a tube, and sanded to a shallow point. (*THE WAYWARD BUS* by John Steinbeck)

CURVING: LIKE A SNAKE: TRAIL: (PLACE) snake-like (Unknown)

CUT OFF: LIKE PEDESTAL: HILL: (PLACE) Gray-colored woods covered a large part of the island. This even tint was broken up by streaks of yellow sand-break in the lower lands, and by many tall pine trees out-topping the others—some singly, some in clumps; but the general coloring was uniform. The hills ran up clear above the vegetation in spires of naked rock. All were strangely shaped, and the Spyglass, which was by three or four hundred feet the tallest on the island, was likewise the strangest in configuration, running up sheer from almost every side, and then suddenly cut off at the top like a pedestal. (*TREASURE ISLAND* by Robert Louis Stevenson)

CUT OUT: LIKE CANCER: (PERSON) Cut the conversation out [of the taped interview] like a malignant cancer. (*DAN BONGINO PODCAST* 20Dec2023)

CUT THROUGH: LIKE HARVESTER IN WHEAT FIELD: (THING) Ground-attack fighters cut through the tank column like a harvester through a wheat-field. It was horrible. (*RED STORM RISING* by Tom Clancy)

DANGEROUS: LIKE SNAKE: (PERSON) dangerous—moved like a snake when it strikes (*THE SECRET WAYS* by Alstair MacLean)

DARK: LIKE LOOKING THROUGH SUN GLASSES: (THING) The darkness, which was like looking through extra-strong sun glasses, seems to have pervaded the world at this hour. Phlegon wrote that in the fourth year of the two hundred and second Olympiad, there was a great darkness over Europe, surpassing anything that had ever been seen. "At midday," he said, "the stars could be seen. At the same time an earthquake caused much damage in Nicaea. Tertullian said later that he found in the records of Rome a notation of worldwide darkness which the statesmen of the Empire could not explain. Apparently the people of Jerusalem were accustomed to sudden changes in the weather, or there would have been a wide sense of alarm or wonder at this time. (THE DAY CHRIST DIED by Jim Bishop)

DARKNESS FOLDED: LIKE WINGS OF BAT: (THING) The darkness folded around them again like the wings of a great bat. (Unknown)

DAWN UPON: FEMALE: WOMAN: (PERSON) The girl had dawned upon him like a glorious sunrise. (*SUNSET PASS* by Zane Grey)

DAYLIGHT SHIFTED: LIKE SOOT OVER STREET: (THING) The gray winter daylight shifted like soot over the gray uptown street. *(STRANGERS* by Dean R. Koontz)

DEAL WITH STAFF: LIKE MAGICIAN: (PERSON) He was picked for his job because he was smart and focused and dealt with his staff like a magician with his deck of cards. (*POWER PLAY* by Catherine Coulter)

DECEIVE: LIKE RED HERRING: (PERSON) ... like a red herring—designed to mislead (Unknown)

DECLINE: LIKE PEOPLE: VILLAGE (PLACE) Communities, like people, have periods of health and times of sickness—even in youth and age, hope and despondency. [There was] a snake of population crawling out from the city... passing ... by, leaving it to its memories. Those remaining persuaded themselves that they liked it that way. They were spared the noise and litter of summer people, the garish glow of neon signs, the spending of tourist money and tourist razzle-dazzle. The snake of population continued to writhe out and everyone knew that sooner or later it would affect the village. The local people longed for that and hated the idea of it at the same time. The neighboring towns were rich, spilled over with loot from tourists, puffed with spoils, gleamed with the great houses of the rich. The village talked of the old days and ... *(THE WINTER OF OUR DISCONTENT* by John Steinbeck*)*

DEMOLISH: LIKE BRICK WALL: (PERSON) We can plod along and hope for a break. But give us one solid fact and we'll bring the whole world down on them. It's like taking down a brick wall. The hard part is getting that first brick loose. (*PATRIOT GAMES* by Tom Clancy)

DEPEND: LIKE SUCCESSFUL ARMY: (THING) An economy, like a successful army, depends on faith and courage. *(SUCCESS*, November 1987*)*

DEPTH CHANGE: LIKE CRIPPLED WHALE: (THING) She changed depth like a crippled whale. Slow going up, even slower going down. *(THE HUNT FOR RED OCTOBER* by Tom Clancy*)*

DERANGED: LIKE CRAZY MAN: (PERSON) He was like a crazy man. (*HEARTLAND* by Bethany Campbell)

DESCEND: LIKE LOCUSTS: (PERSON) they descended upon the stores like a plague of locusts. (Unknown)

DESPAIR: EYES: LIKE COLD HORROR: (PERSON) Despair came into her eyes, like a cold horror, and her cheeks and mouth sagged and the muscles of her shoulders and arms collapsed. (*THE DAY CHRIST WAS BORN* by Jim Bishop)

DIDACTIC VOICE: LIKE LECTURING COLLEGE PROFESSOR: (PERSON) The attorney tapped his fingers on the arms of his power chair, *tap, tap, tap,* thinking hard. Finally he spoke, his voice didactic, like a college professor lecturing a roomful of students. (*RECKONING* by Catherine Coulter)

DIG IN: LIKE CAT: (PERSON) digging in his heels like a cat in a sandbox. (Unknown)

DISAPPEAR: LIKE BAD GUYS: (PERSON) The shooters had disappeared. It was like the bad guys jumped in a hole and pulled it in behind them. (*PATRIOT GAMES* by Tom Clancy)

DISAPPEAR: LIKE SMOKE IN A WIND: (THING) The voice sounded in her mind again, sharp, vicious, and then it disappeared like smoke in a wind. (*RECKONING* by Catherine Coulter)

DISBELIEF: LIKE DOUBTING THOMAS: (THING) ... like a doubting Thomas. *(THE GRAPES OF WRATH* by John Steinbeck*)*

DISCARD: LIKE KLEENEX: (PERSON) They were going to throw him away like a used Kleenex. (*THE CARDINAL OF THE KREMLIN* by Tom Clancy)

DISCARD: LIKE PAPER: (PERSON) Discard her like a Saturday paper on Sunday morning. (Unknown)

THE METAPHORS OF LIKE 33

DISCONTENTED: LIKE DOG IN TRAP: (PERSON) He appeared what he had become—sullen, conceited, resentful, remote and secret in the pain and perplexity of his pubescence, a dreadful, harrowing time when he must bite everyone near, even himself, like a dog in a trap—a miserable discontent. (*THE WINTER OF OUR DISCONTENT* by John Steinbeck)

DISOLVE: LIKE SNOW: (PERSON) His troubles melted away like snow in the spring. (Unknown)

DISSOLVE: LIKE SNOW: (PERSON) "The earth shall soon dissolve like snow." (*hymn AMAZING GRACE*)

DISSOLVE: LIKE SNOW: (THING) the earth shall soon dissolve like snow... (Christian *HYMN* "Amazing Grace")

DISTEND: LIKE BLOWN UP RUBBER GLOVE: (PERSON) Then he became rigid with tension. His body seemed distended, like a blown up rubber glove. (*THE WAYWARD BUS* by John Steinbeck)

DIVE: LIKE CASE: (PERSON) He liked to dive headfirst into a case like this. (*POWER PLAY* by Catherine Coulter)

DIVIDE: LIKE PART IN HAIR: (THING) July parts the year like the part in a head of hair. *(THE WINTER OF OUR DISCONTENT* by John Steinbeck)

DIVORCED: LIKE SISTER: (PERSON) The room door opened and three men marched in; in the lead was a white-haired gentleman wearing a bespoke gray wool suit and a matching dark blue tie, a man whose manicurist probably came to his office weekly to tend to his finger-nails. The second man was a younger clone of the first. The third man wasn't a lawyer. He was forty, married and divorced three times like his sister. He had three children, all living with their mothers, all out of state. (*RECKONING* by Catherine Coulter)

DRAWING: DREAMLIKE QUALITY: (THING) The beautiful drawing had a rapt, dreamlike quality as if she had simply translated a vision that sprang unbidden to her mind. (*INSIGHT* Article by Jane Addams Allen)

DRAWN TO: LIKE MOTH: (PERSON) ... drawn to it like a moth to a flame. (Unknown)

DREAM WAFT AWAY: LIKE MORNING MIST: (PERSON) When he awoke, the dreams of a peaceful contented life wafted away from his grasp like the morning mist. (*THE CARDINAL OF THE KREMLIN* by Tom Clancy)

DRESSED UP: LIKE HER: (PERSON) Like Emma, he dressed up a bit, probably forced to by his parents, in black chinos and a dark green sweater. Not sneakers, but polished boots on his feet. (*RECKONING* by Catherine Coulter)

DRIFT: LIKE GHOST: (PERSON) she drifted around like a ghost out of the lost legion of the damned. (*HEARTLAND* by Bethany Campbell)

DRINK: LIKE BEER: (PERSON) ... gin and tonic. I rattled the ice and drank if down like beer and felt its dry heat reach out over my shoulders and down my arms so that my skin shimmered. (*THE WINTER OF OUR DISCONTENT* by John Steinbeck)

DRINK: LIKE HORSE: (PERSON) His huge companion dropped his blankets and flung himself down and drank from the surface of the green pool, drank with long gulps, snorting into the water like a horse. The small man stepped nervously beside him. (*OF MICE AND MEN* by John Steinbeck)

DRINKING OIL: LIKE GOPHER HOLE: (THING) "Them [cylinder] walls can take it. She's drinkin' oil like a gopher hole awready. Little more ain't gonna hurt none." He worked the rod over the shaft and the lower half. "She'll take some shim." he said. "Casy!" "Yeah" "I'm takin' up this here bearing now. Get out to that crank an' turn her over slow when I tell ya." He tightened the bolts. "Now. Over slow!" And as the angular shaft turned, he worked the bearing against it. "Too much shim," Tom said. "Hold it, Casy." He took out the bolts and removed thin shims from each side and put the bolts back in. "Try her again, Casy!" And he worked the rod again. "She's a little bit loose yet. Wonder if she'd be too tight if I took out more shim. I'll try her." Again he removed the bolts and took out another pair of thin strips. "Now try her, Casy." "That looks good." Will I think she's snug here. He tapped the cotter pins in and bent the ends out. Casy knelt down and took the flashlight. He kept the beam on the working hands as they patted the gasket gently in place and lined the holes with the pan bolts. The two men strained at the weight of the pan, caught the end bolts, and then set in the others; and when they were all engaged, Tom took them up little by little until the pan settled evenly in against the gasket, and he tightened hard against the nuts. He tightened the oil tap, looked carefully up at the pan, and took the light and searched the ground. "There she is. Let's get the oil back in her." They poured the bucket of oil back in the crank case and Tom inspected the gasket for leaks. "O.K., Al. Turn her over," he said. Al got into the car and stepped on the starter. The motor caught with a roar. Blue smoke poured from the exhaust pipes. "Throttle down!" Tom shouted. "She'll burn oil till that wire goes. Gettin' thinner now." And as the motor turned over, he listened carefully. "Put up the spark an' let her idle." He listened again. "O.K., Al. Turn her off. I think we done her." *(THE GRAPES OF WRATH* by John Steinbeck*)*

DRIVE THEM: LIKE SLAVES: (PERSON) drove them like slaves. (*HEARTLAND* by Bethany Campbell)

DRIZZLED INTO CANYON: LIKE MELTED BUTTER INTO CLEFT OF LOAF OF BREAD: (THING) the sun drizzled light into the yawning canyon like melted butter into the crusty cleft of a loaf of bread (Unknown)

DROP ARMS: LIKE DEFLATED BALLOON: (PERSON) She held the canister over the screaming man's pain-knotted face, and depressed the nozzle. A fine, nearly invisible mist hissed out of the canister. The thug raised his hands in front of his face in a warding-off gesture, his eyes wide, white, and bulging. Then his arms dropped like deflated balloons and his features went slack and he fell off into sedated unconsciousness. (*POWER PLAYS POLITIKA* by Tom Clancy and Martin Greenberg)

DROP INTO SLEEP: LIKE STONE: (PERSON) She slept deeply for two hours, dropping into oblivion like a stone in a pool, and staying deep at the bottom. When she woke she had her warm blanket wrapped tightly around. (*MIDNIGHT SHADOWS* by Nora Roberts)

DROP: LIKE HOT POTATO: (PERSON) dropped like a hot potato. (*THE DAN BONGINO SHOW* 1 March 2024)

DROP: LIKE ROCK: (PERSON) It was like dropping a rock in a pond. (Unknown)

DUST SETTLED: LIKE POLLEN: HOUSES: (THING) Now the dust was evenly mixed with the air, an emulsion of dust and air. Houses were shut tight, and cloth wedged around doors and windows, but the dust came in so thinly that it could not be seen in the air, and it settled like pollen on the chairs and tables, on the dishes. The people brushed it from their shoulders. Little lines of dust lay at the door sills. Men and women huddled in their houses, and they tied handkerchiefs over their noses when they went out, and wore goggles to protect their eyes. (*THE GRAPES OF WRATH* by John Steinbeck)

EAT MEN: LIKE WOLF EATS RABBITS: (THING) The battle was turning into a living thing that ate men and tanks like a wolf eats rabbits. (*RED STORM RISING* by Tom Clancy)

EAT: LIKE BULL: (PERSON) He was in magnificent health and spirits, eating like a bull, sleeping like a tree, yet he would not enjoy a moment until he heard his old tarpaulin, tramping round the capstans. (*TREASURE ISLAND* by Robert Louis Stevenson)

ECHO SOUND: LIKE DISTANT THUNDER: (THING) The sound echoed through the steel hull like distant thunder. (*RED STORM RISING* by Tom Clancy)

EJECTION SOUND: LIKE TRUCK AIR BRAKE: **(THING)** The submarine shuddered as the [missile] was ejected upward by the gas charge. The sound was like a truck's air brake. (*THE HUNT FOR RED OCTOBER* by Tom Clancy)

ELECTION: LIKE SHAKING SNOW GLOBE: (THING) ... the Iowa caucus is like shaking a snow globe — everything is up in the air again. (Unknown)

ELECTIONS: LIKE MARRIAGES: (THING) Political elections... are a good deal like marriages, there's no accounting for anyone's taste. (Will Rogers)

EMERGE: LIKE SOMETHING FROM NIGHTMARE: (THING) The main battle tanks emerged from the woods like something from a nightmare, their long cannon belching flame as they glided across the rolling ground. (*RED STORM RISING* by Tom Clancy)

EMOTION: LIKE FACE: (PERSON) His mind and his emotions were like his face, constantly erupting, constantly raw and irritated. He had times of violent purity when he howled at his own depravity, and these were usually followed by a melancholy laziness that all but prostrated him, and he went from the depression into sleep. It was operatic and left him drugged and dull for a long time. (*THE WAYWARD BUS* by John Steinbeck)

ENCIRCLE: LIKE STEEL BANDS: (PERSON) Arms encircled her suddenly like steel bands. (*LOVE UPON THE WIND* by Sally Stewart)

ENERGY: LIKE PALPABLE FORCE: (THING) like a palpable force of energy. (*HEARTLAND* by Bethany Campbell)

ESCAPE: LIKE SPOTTED ARROW: DOG: (THING) The minute the back door was opened, it was off like a spotted arrow. (*JEWELS OF THE SUN* by Nora Roberts)

ETCHED: LIKE WORK OF ART: STREET: (PLACE) I have walked these streets my whole life, I know them just the same as if they were etched in my head with a sharp knife, scored in deep like some strange work of art. These are the streets I grew up on and for the most part I'm calm here, at home, on the down low with a steady heartbeat. Not tonight though. Tonight my heart wants out of my chest. It wants to beat free of its cage. It pounds like it's going to crack a rib. My senses are on high alert. Every color is brighter, every noise louder, every stranger a cause to make my heart beat more fiercely still. It's been like that since the bikers came to town, marking out their turf like a wolf pack. I don't even deal drugs but they mean to dominate everyone regardless. They've got Kenny dealing for them already, there goes his grades, and there goes his life. So now the streets that were my salvation spike my adrenaline as good as a shot to the arm. (Unknown)

EXAMINE: LIKE TISSUE CULTURE: (PERSON) Being examined by senior officials like a tissue culture on a Petri dish could make you old rather quickly. (*RED STORM RISING* by Tom Clancy)

EXCITED: LIKE BIRD: (PERSON) Excitement took wings within her, beating like a bird in her breast. (*COUNTRY OF THE HEART* by Robyn Donald)

EXPLODE: LIKE FLASHBULB: (PERSON) His remark exploded like a flashbulb in front of his eyes. (*PATRIOT GAMES* by Tom Clancy)

EXPLOSION: LIKE LOUD STRING OF FIRECRACKERS: (THING) Four canisters of cluster bombs fell, splitting open in the air. A small cloud of bomblets cascaded on the observation post. Even from three miles away, it sounded like a loud string of firecrackers as the hilltop post disappeared in a cloud of dust and sparks. (*RED STORM RISING* by Tom Clancy)

EXTEND: LIKE PEPPERMINT STICK: (PERSON) She wondered how long she could make the day last. Like a peppermint stick, she would hold onto today until she got another one as good. (*THE WAYWARD BUS* by John Steinbeck)

EYEBROWS OVERHANG: LIKE DOG: (PERSON) A tall, stooped old man opened the door to the lunchroom, came in, and sat down on a stool. He had his head bent permanently forward on the arthritic stalk of his neck so that the tip of his nose pointed straight at the ground. He was well over sixty, and his eyebrows overhung his eyes like those of a Skye terrier. His long, deeply channeled upper lip was raised over his teeth like he little trunk of a tapir. The point over his middle teeth seemed to be almost prehensile. His eyes were yellowish gold, so that he looked fierce. (*THE WAYWARD BUS* by John Steinbeck)

EYEBROWS: LIKE FINGERNAILS: ROADSIDE: (PLACE) The sun lay on the grass and warmed it, and in the shade under the grass the insects moved, ants and ant lions to set traps for them, grasshoppers to jump into the air and flick their yellow wings for a second, sow bugs like little armadillos, plodding restlessly on many tender feet. And over the grass at the roadside a land turtle crawled, turning aside for nothing, dragging his high-domed shell over the grass. His hard legs and yellow-nailed feet threshed slowly through the grass, not really walking, but boosting and dragging his shell along. The barley beads slid off his shell, and the clover burrs fell on him and rolled to the ground. His horny beak was partly open, and his fierce, humorous eyes, under brows like fingernails, stared straight ahead. He came over the grass leaving a beaten trail behind him, and the hill, which was the highway embankment, reared up ahead of him. For a moment he stopped, his head held high. He blinked and looked up and down. At last he started to climb the embankment. Front clawed feet reached forward but did not touch. The hind feet kicked his shell along, and it scraped on the grass, and on the gravel. As the embankment grew steeper and steeper, the more frantic were the efforts of the land turtle. Pushing hind legs strained and slipped, boosting the shell along, and the horny head protruded as far as the neck could stretch. Little by little the shell slid up the embankment until at last a parapet cut straight across its line of march, the shoulder of the road, a concrete wall four inches high. *(THE GRAPES OF WRATH by John Steinbeck)*

EYES WIDE: LIKE RABBIT: (PERSON) Her feedback was inspiring. "Look, honey, you keep your eyes too wide, like a rabbit. Just let your upper lids droop down a little bit. There, like that. Now look at yourself and see the difference. (*THE DAY CHRIST WAS BO*RN by Jim Bishop)

EYES: LIKE CAVES: (PERSON) He was in a towering rage. He arose from his couch, a man with deep-set eyes like caves in a forest, and his gray beard parted and his tongue spat words of anger. His rage enslaved him and he tore fabrics and drapes from the walls and screamed until the saliva hung on his beard. (*THE DAY CHRIST WAS BORN* by Jim Bishop)

EYES: LIKE DEEP WELL OF BLACK: ACTION: (PERSON) He was breathing hard as he stepped back. His teeth looked discolored. He looked much older than his fifty-six years. His graying brown hair was thin on his head, a gray stubble dotted his sagging jowls. He looked like a harmless old dude, except for his eyes. Even from twelve feet away, she saw madness in him, bursting to get out. His eyes looked like a deep well of black, and behind those eyes crouched scary things. (*POWER PLAY* by Catherine Coulter)

EYES: LIKE DISINTERESTED MAN: (PERSON) The interrogator who entered was about forty and well dressed in civilian clothes. He carried a few sheets of paper. The man walked around to the far side of the table, and didn't look at the courier until he sat down. When he did look at him, his eyes were disinterested, like a man at the zoo examining a creature from a distant land. (*THE CARDINAL OF THE KREMLIN* by Tom Clancy)

EYES: LIKE MOTHER: (PERSON) Those eyes, so much like her mother's, gleamed behind the sheen of tears. (*ABANDONED IN DEATH* by J. D. Robb)

EYES: LIKE PUPPY: (PERSON) His eyes were bright and questioning, like a puppy's eyes. (*THE WAYWARD BUS* by John Steinbeck)

EYES: LIKE SAUCER: (PERSON) he was a natural clown, physically comic with a short, stout figure, bald head, and saucer-like brown eyes. (*CIRCLE OF FATE* by Charlotte Lamb)

EYES: LIKE WOLF: (PERSON) His eyes were long and narrow and slanted like the eyes of a sleepy wolf. (*THE WAYWARD BUS* by John Steinbeck)

FACADE: LIKE IT GREW OUT OF GROUND: (PLACE) The ledge was more like a rocky outcrop, rustic and rough. It was in keeping with the building, only three years old but made to look as if it were ancient. The rocks had been trucked in from some quarry up north and the builders had to consult with old-fashioned brick layers to get the rock facade right. It was all steel and concrete underneath of course, but from out here it looked like it just grew right out of the ground. On the ledge should have been pigeons, peering down in the way they do, looking for pedestrians dropping fragments of their breakfasts. But in the frosted dawn-light the ledge is layered with roses, red, white and pink. It could be a romantic gesture from some eccentric billionaire, but it isn't. It's one rose for day of the empresses' life... (Unknown)

FACE: DELICATE: LIKE DOLL: (PERSON) lovely face that was curiously doll-like in its delicacy and would have looked more natural within the pages of a fashion magazine. (*FEAR THE DARK* by Kay Hooper)

FACE: LIKE BATTERED SHOE: (PERSON) He had a face like an old battered shoe, not to mention one cast eye. (*STRANGERS* by Dean R. Koontz)

FACE: LIKE FOX: (PERSON) For one small second, he thought he'd felt eyes on his face. Then he noticed the agent who had been posted at the entrance to the waiting area start walking in his direction. The man had bristle-cut hair and a pointed, vigilant face ... like a fox. (*POWER PLAYS POLITIKA* by Tom Clancy and Martin Greenberg)

FACE: LIKE MINIATURE PORTRAIT: (PERSON) her face alone was standing out against a grey and misty background, like some miniature portrait. (*THE CAPTAIN FROM CONNECTICUT* by C.S. Forester)

FACE: LIKE NOVEL: (PERSON) His face was like a Stephen King novel. (Unknown)

FACE: LOOKED LIKE OATMEAL: (PERSON) She stood naked in front of her bathroom mirror, staring at the bright purple bruises on her arms, her shoulders, and her chest. She looked over her shoulder, and saw her back looked like a multicolor flag and the bruise on her butt something like Australia. The face in the mirror staring back at her looked like oatmeal. (*VORTEX* by Catherine Coulter)

FACE: SHARP: LIKE PUPPY: (PERSON) His face was sharp, like a puppy's face. (*THE WAYWARD BUS* by John Steinbeck)

FACE: SLICK OF FEAR: (PERSON) He remembered the local teenagers, probably there on a bet, to gawk at that awesome house, remembered how afraid they were that they might get caught. He'd always liked that slick of fear he saw on all those faces. (*POWER PLAY* by Catherine Coulter)

FACEBOOK: LIKE GALLOPING DOG: (THING) Facebook is a bit like that big dog galloping toward you in the park. You're not sure if he wants to play with you or eat you (*FORTUNE DATA SHEET*)

FACT CHECK: LIKE VAMPIRE BAT: (PERSON) They followed every word he spoke like blood-sucking vampire bats so they could change the narrative. (*THE DAN BONGINO SHOW* October 27, 2022)

FADE: LIKE GRASS: (THING) life is a vapor like the grass of the field and the flower that fades—here for a short time (then gone) to eternity. (Amir Tsarfati, *BEHOLD ISRAEL*, 23Apr2024)

FAILURE: LIKE SAND TRAP: (PERSON) Failure is a state of mind. It's like one of those sand traps an ant lion digs. You keep sliding back. It takes one hell of a jump to get out of this mindset. Once you get out, you find success is a state of mind too. (*THE WINTER OF OUR DISCONTENT* by John Steinbeck)

FALL: ACTION: SPIN: (PERSON) In a mad dance, she spin across the sand, above it, her arms spread like wings, her hair falling in coils, like snakes. (*HEAVEN AND EARTH* by Nora Roberts)

FALL: LIKE CLOAK: (PERSON) ... car had taken 14 hours and 400 miles to reach their destination cold and hungry and exhausted; once they were inside the safety and shelter of the house, these things fell from them like a cloak. (*THE SECRET WAYS* by Alstair MacLean)

FALL: LIKE RAIN: (PERSON) bitter tears fell like rain from the young man's eyes ... (*THE CARDINAL OF THE KREMLIN* by Tom Clancy)

FALLING SNOWFLAKES: LIKE FAT, WET ASTERISKS: (THING) snowflakes falling like fat, wet asterisks (Unknown)

FAMILY: LIKE GRAPE PLANTS: (PERSON) Families are like grape plants in full leaf, laden with plump berries hanging heavy, looking rich and beautiful. They are nothing though, without the thick, strong vine hidden below, holding them up and giving them life. Families are the vine holding us up, filling us with love, dependability, and strength so we can go it alone facing the world, leading with the branches of family around us. (*PORTALS OF PRAYER* April – June 2024)

FEEL ANGER: LIKE SUDDEN STORM: PERSON: ... fits of anger came like sudden storms at sea. (*THE LIVING REED* by Pearl S. Buck)

FEEL BRAVE: LIKE SIR GALAHAD: (PERSON) He felt like Sir Galahad wanting to fight dragons and then lay them at her feet. She had moved him, possessed him, and made him see himself in a different light. (*QUINN* by Iris Johansen)

FEEL CAUGHT: LIKE FLY: (PERSON) She felt like a fly caught in a web, unable to move let alone escape. (Unknown)

FEEL DARKNESS: LIKE SHADOWS: (PERSON) She sensed a darkness moving beneath the surface of the conversation, more secrets that swam like shadows in the depths of things. (*HEARTLAND* by Bethany Campbell)

FEEL DIGGING: LIKE TICK: (PERSON) Something was digging on him like a tick under his skin. (Unknown)

FEEL EMOTION: LIKE ANTI-SMOKING ACTIVIST: (PERSON) <name> suddenly felt like someone who'd found religion, or gone from being a three-pack-a-day smoker to being an anti-tobacco activist. (*POWER PLAYS POLITIKA* by Tom Clancy and Martin Greenberg)

FEEL EMOTION: LIKE FIRST CRUSH: (PERSON) The emotion made him feel like a cross between a knight in shining armor and a kid with his first crush. (*QUINN* by Iris Johansen)

FEEL EMOTION: LIKE FOUND RELIGION: (PERSON) <name> suddenly felt like someone who'd found religion, or gone from being a three-pack-a-day smoker to being an anti-tobacco activist. (*POWER PLAYS POLITIKA* by Tom Clancy and Martin Greenberg)

FEEL EMOTION: LIKE KNIGHT: (PERSON) The emotion made him feel like a cross between a knight in shining armor and a kid with his first crush. (*QUINN* by Iris Johansen)

FEEL EVIL: LIKE SHADOWS: (PERSON) She stopped when she felt the air change—from light and fresh to heavy and dark. She saw movement through the slits of windows, through the wide opening—like shadows shifting and sliding. (*THE BECOMING* by Nora Roberts)

FEEL EXHAUSTED: LIKE WIRES: (PERSON) Her eyes burned, begged to shut down for just a few minutes. The back of her neck felt like wires hummed and twisted under her skin. (*DESPERATION IN DEATH* by J.D. Robb)

FEEL FEAR: LIKE BLOW: (PERSON) The panic on the young woman's face struck him like a blow. Those already enormous silver-gray eyes had widened more with fear while her face had grown even paler. (*AGENT TO THE RESCUE* by Lisa Childs)

FEEL FEAR: LIKE FLAMES: (PERSON) The priests were afraid that at any moment something magical would happen, like flames leaping out of the flagstones or unheralded claps of thunder. (*THE DAY CHRIST DIED* by Jim Bishop)

FEEL FEAR: LIKE PEACH PIT: (PERSON) She wished she didn't sometimes feel that fear rolling around like a peach pit in her belly. (RECKONING by Catherine Coulter)

FEEL FEAR: LIKE THUNDER: (PERSON) The priests were afraid that at any moment something magical would happen, like flames leaping out of the flagstones or unheralded claps of thunder. (*THE DAY CHRIST DIED* by Jim Bishop)

FEEL FREE: LIKE BALLOON: (PERSON) felt like a balloon that had become untethered and now could drift away into the sky. (Unknown)

FEEL FREE: LIKE CAGED BIRD: (PERSON) We nudged our way in the damp segmented worms of traffic, feeling a little grand and helpless and lost, like cage-bred birds set free, and frightened as freedom shows its teeth. (*THE WINTER OF OUR DISCONTENT* by John Steinbeck)

FEEL GOOD: LIKE CAKE ICING: (PERSON) ... was like icing on the cake (Unknown)

FEEL HEADACHE: LIKE SOGGY APPLE: (PERSON) His head felt like a soggy apple full of worms. (ABANDONED IN DEATH by J. D. Robb)

FEEL HEARTBURN: LIKE DISCOMFORT: (PERSON) like the discomfort of heartburn. (Unknown)

FEEL HEAT: LIKE NEW YORK NOR'EASTER: (PERSON) It felt like New York in a heat wave, facing down an early nor'easter. There was high humidity, and a big threat of rain. (*THE LAST SECOND* by Catherine Coulter)

FEEL HOPE: LIKE GLIMMER OF LIGHT: (PERSON) It was like a glimmer of light beyond the darkness. (Unknown)

FEEL INSINCERE: LIKE FISH: (PERSON) ... like a Mackerel in the moonlight—it shined but it still stunk. (Unknown)

FEEL LIKE: ACTION: HOLD: (PERSON) The hands holding his felt like bony feathers. (*NIGHTWORK* by Nora Roberts)

FEEL LIKE: BEER TOSSED IN FACE: (PERSON) The threat in the graffiti was obvious, but she felt it was silly. No one would get his nose out of joint that much and it didn't feel like a beer tossed in her face or a threat to pull her tonsils out through her ear. (*POWER PLAY* by Catherine Coulter)

FEEL LIKE: THREAT: (PERSON) The threat in the graffiti was obvious, but she felt it was silly. No one would get his nose out of joint that much and it didn't feel like a beer tossed in her face or a threat to pull her tonsils out through her ear. (*POWER PLAY* by Catherine Coulter)

FEEL LOSS: LIKE RIP INTO HEART: (PERSON) His thumb traced the back of her hand, then he quickly released it, and she felt the loss of contact like a rip into her heart. (*UNDETECTED* by Dee Henderson)

FEEL MAN: LIKE HIM: (PERSON) In her final moments of consciousness, she could feel him behind her, flesh and bone like her. Except he was dark, something once human, but coated in darkness like a sledge of evil. He was strong—so strong. And he was cold, and inescapable. She tried to force words past the forearm pressed against her throat, but couldn't. She didn't really feel the knife, not immediately. Just his forearm removed, and before she could say anything at all, there was something else preventing her from speaking. She put her hands up and felt the horrendous opening of her throat, felt the hot blood flowing over her hands, and her legs went weak. She stumbled ahead toward the light she could see ahead on the street. Light that was dimming with every staggering step she took. Her life flowed out redly between her fingers. (*FEAR THE DARK* by Kay Hooper)

FEEL MAN: LIKE SLEDGE OF EVIL: (PERSON) In her final moments of consciousness, she could feel him behind her, flesh and bone like her. Except he was dark, something once human, but coated in darkness like a sledge of evil. He was strong—so strong. And he was cold, and inescapable. She tried to force words past the forearm pressed against her throat, but couldn't. She didn't really feel the knife, not immediately. Just his forearm removed, and before she could say anything at all, there was something else preventing her from speaking. She put her hands up and felt the horrendous opening of her throat, felt the hot blood flowing over her hands, and her legs went weak. She stumbled ahead toward the light she could see ahead on the street. Light that was dimming with every staggering step she took. Her life flowed out redly between her fingers. (*FEAR THE DARK* by Kay Hooper)

FEEL MOVEMENT: LIKE FLY: (PERSON) "high speed travel – he felt like a fly on the nose of a bullet." (*THE 2019 OLD FARMER'S ALMANAC*)

FEEL OUT OF CONTROL: LIKE CAUGHT: (PERSON) He felt like he was caught in some colossal machine, one that was running down and down beyond control. (*POWER PLAYS POLITIKA* by Tom Clancy and Martin Greenberg)

FEEL OVERWHELMED: LIKE TOSSED ON STAGE: (PERSON) For a moment, Molly couldn't take it in. She felt like she'd been tossed on a stage in the middle of a bizarre play and didn't know her lines. (*RECKONING* by Catherine Coulter)

FEEL PAIN: LIKE ACID: (PERSON) She wanted the pain to go away, to not continue to eat like an acid into the fabric of her life. (*COUNTRY OF THE HEART* by Robyn Donald)

FEEL PAIN: LIKE HOT POKERS: (PERSON) When he was shot, the pain was incredible, like hot pokers shoving into him over and over. (*THE LAST SECOND* by Catherine Coulter)

FEEL PAIN: LIKE MEGAPHONE ROUSING WORLD: (PERSON) pain shouted out like a megaphone trying to rouse a deaf world, insisting it be heard and attended to. (*KOINIONA HOUSE* article by Ron Matsen)

FEEL PANIC: LIKE ANIMAL CLAWING: (PERSON) Panic came upon him like an animal clawing at his throat. (*MIDNIGHT SHADOWS* by Nora Roberts)

FEEL PANIC: LIKE BRUSH FIRE: (PERSON) Panic raced throughout ... like brush fire through a parched wood. (*DAILY RECKONING*, 8/10/2018)

FEEL PANIC: LIKE FLUTTERING BIRD: (PERSON) Melissa could feel Cassie's panic, like the fluttering of a captured bird. (*FINAL TARGET* by Iris Johansen)

FEEL PLEASURE: LIKE RIP-TIDE: (PERSON) Pleasure was surging through her body like a rip-tide. (*LOVE UPON THE WIND* by Sally Stewart)

FEEL PRESENCE: LIKE WARM BLANKET: (PERSON) Hearing him singing in the kitchen, she found his presence like a warm blanket on a chilly morning. (*THE BECOMING* by Nora Roberts)

FEEL ROUGH: LIKE OLD BARK: (PERSON) ... rough like old bark. (Author)

FEEL ROUGH: LIKE SANDPAPER: (PERSON) like sandpaper (Unknown)

FEEL SILENCE: LIKE FINE DUST: (PERSON) felt the silence in the house settle like fine dust on her; her spirits sank. (*CIRCLE OF FATE* by Charlotte Lamb)

FEEL STRETCHED: LIKE SCRAPED BUTTER: (PERSON) "I feel thin, sort of stretched, like butter scraped over too much bread." (*THE FELLOWSHIP OF THE RING* by J.R.R. Tolkien)

FEEL TACTICS: LIKE PLAYING CHESS: (PERSON) "It feels like the Democrats have been playing chess and we've been playing checkers." (Unknown)

FEEL THWACK: LIKE ROD: (PERSON) It was completely dark inside the den. He heard a low predatory rumble. Soft, padded

THE METAPHORS OF LIKE

footsteps passed by him, and coarse wisps of hair brushed against his arm. His left leg suddenly buckled after what felt like a rod thwacked into his thigh. A second hit helped him to identify it as an agitated tail swishing side to side. (*DISCOVERING DANIEL* by Amir Tsarfati)

FEEL TIRED: LIKE UNWOUND CLOCK: (PERSON) He was so weary he had energy like an unwound clock. (Readers Digest *TOWARD MORE PICTURESQUE SPEECH*)

FEEL UNINFORMED: LIKE MUSHROOM: (PERSON) ... felt like a mushroom growing in the dark (Unknown)

FEEL WELCOME: LIKE THOUSAND WELCOMES: (PERSON) "...it felt like a thousand [welcomes] when she stepped into the warmth [of the house] (*JEWELS OF THE SUN* by Nora Roberts)

FEEL WINTER: LIKE BEING FIRST: (PERSON) felt a curious excitement waling the new unmarked snow or frost; like being first in a new world, a deep, satisfying sense of discovery of something clean and new, unused and un-dirtied. (*THE WINTER OF OUR DISCONTENT* by John Steinbeck)

FEEL: (PERSON) Overheard at a cocktail party "I feel more like I do now, than I did when I came in". (Unknown)

FEEL: EMBARRASSED: PERSON:... felt like she would die of embarrassment. (Unknown)

FEEL: LIKE BEING WATCHED: (PERSON) It was like being watched by some streamlined golden bird of prey. (*HEARTLAND* by Bethany Campbell)

FEEL: LIKE DEAD MAN: (PERSON) He felt like a dead man going through the motions of being alive. (*LOVE UPON THE WIND* by Sally Stewart)

FEEL: LIKE FLAMES: ANGRY EYES: (PERSON) He felt their hot angry eyes upon him like flames. (*THE LIVING REED* by Pearl S. Buck)

FEEL: LIKE GELETIN: (PERSON) The two faced each other with guns drawn. The air around them felt like gelatin infused with current. He was unaware of the sudden movement behind him until it was too late. It all seemed to happen with lightning rapidity-the oiled click of a firing mechanism near his ear, the loud crack of the gun discharging behind him, the surprised, almost quizzical expression on her face just before the bullet struck her forehead, producing a perfectly round dot of red above the ridge of her nose, and for a heart-stopping instant was sure her finger would spasmodically lock around the trigger, sure he would be blown off his feet. But the weapon slipped from her grasp without firing a round, and then her eyes rolled up in their sockets and her legs gave out and she slid loosely to the floor, trailing blood, brains, and skull fragments down the wall as she crumpled. (*POWER PLAYS POLITIKA* by Tom Clancy and Martin Greenberg)

FEEL: LIKE LITTLE PLANT: (PERSON) After she married she felt like a little plant that her husband watered and weeded and dug around, but the mature plant was already implicit in the seedling. (Article by Jane Addams Allen)

FEEL: LIKE PARROT: (PERSON) While he didn't really understand the principles of lasers, he had the engineering details committed to his trained memory. It made him feel like a parrot. He could repeat the words without comprehending its significance. (*THE CARDINAL OF THE KREMLIN* by Tom Clancy)

FEEL: LIKE PING PONG BALL: (PERSON) He felt like a Ping-Pong ball bounced between the two agencies. (*VORTEX* by Catherine Coulter)

FEEL: LIKE SLIPPING INTO PAINTING: (PERSON) She felt like she was slipping into a painting, one animated with the flutter of leaves, the sounds of birds, the smell of wet, growing things. (*JEWELS OF THE SUN* by Nora Roberts)

FEEL: LIKE SMORGASBORD MEAT: (PERSON) Seated beside his wife and daughter on the speaker's platform, while a comedian was snapping off one-liners at the mike, he felt like a cold piece of meat on a makeshift smorgasbord. Any minute now somebody was going to flip the dam platform over on its side and the starving rabble in the audience would feast. (POWER PLAYS POLITIKA by Tom Clancy and Martin Greenberg)

FEEL: LIKE STICKING HEAD OUT WINDOW: (PERSON) The experience is a little like sticking your head out a car window at highway speed. The wind blows so hard you forget to breathe. (*SUCCESS*, November 1987)

FEEL: LIKE SUCCESSFUL ARMY: (PERSON) An economy, like a successful army, depends on faith and courage, (*SUCCESS*, November 1987)

FEEL: LIKE TODDLING CHILD: (PERSON) he felt like a toddling child wandering through a university laboratory and wondering at the pretty lights. (*THE CARDINAL OF THE KREMLIN* by Tom Clancy)

FEEL: LIKE TROOP OF BOY SCOUTS TYING KNOTS IN STOMACH: (PERSON) However remote the possibility, the idea made her feel like an entire troop of Boy Scouts were tying knots in her stomach. (*JEWELS OF THE SUN* by Nora Roberts)

FEEL: LIKE WATER: SLIDE: (PERSON) The anger emptied out of her as quickly as it had filled. The room spun, and she felt her emotions slide down like water from a jar. (*THE BECOMING* by Nora Roberts)

FEEL: LIKE YELLOW TASTE: ANGRY: (PERSON) Hatred was rising in her throat like a yellow taste, more sickening than furious. (*THE WINTER OF OUR DISCONTENT* by John Steinbeck)

FEEL: WRAP IN SOUNDS: LIKE WARM SPA ROBE: (PERSON) He spoke in a cool, upper-class Brit accent that never failed to charm her. She felt she could wallow in those lovely sounds and warp herself in them, like a big warm spa robe. (*POWER PLAY* by Catherine Coulter)

FEELING: LIKE TRIPLE-DECK INSTINCT: (PERSON) Like my triple-deck instincts, I had one this morning. It was real strong, hair on the back of my neck and everything. (*THE WINTER OF OUR DISCONTENT* by John Steinbeck)

FEET IN AIR: LIKE ROADKILL: DOG: (THING) A big yellow dog slept in a patch of sunlight on the side yard. It was on its back with its feet in the air like roadkill. (*JEWELS OF THE SUN* by Nora Roberts)

FERNS: LIKE GREEN FOUNTAINS: FOREST: (PLACE) Smell of damp leaves, splash of water from a stream, cascading over tiny waterfalls, fungus on rotting tree stumps, rustle of roosting birds, wind stirs trees, twigs snapping, curious sounds, eerie noises, owl hoot, hush, whispering trees, ferns like green fountains, crunch of dried bracken underfoot, woodland clearing with purple spikes of Fireweed. (Unknown)

FESTER: LIKE WOUND: (PERSON) [It was] like a wound that never heals, that will fester until he finds a way to make her pay. (*POWER PLAY* by Catherine Coulter)

FIERY BREACH OF HEAT: LIKE EVIL EMANATION: (THING) It had been hot enough in the Land Rover, but the heat outside was like an evil emanation, swallowing them up in its fiery breath. (*COUNTRY OF THE HEART* by Robyn Donald)

FIGHT: LIKE TRAPPED BADGER: (PERSON) ... fought like a trapped badger. (Author)

FILL CURTAINS: LIKE SAILS: BEDROOM: (PLACE) The red dots were swimming on my eyes, and the street light threw the shadows of naked elm branches on the ceiling, where they made slow and stately cats' cradles because the spring wind was blowing. The window was open halfway and the white curtains swelled and filled like sails on an anchored boat. I didn't want to go back to sleep. I wanted to go on full tasting how good I felt. (*THE WINTER OF OUR DISCONTENT* by John Steinbeck)

FILTERING LIGHT: LIKE STAINED GLASS: RIVER: (PLACE) The river has a strength that is reflected in the trees. It flows on with confidence, taking the form of the river bed, billions of drops moving together. The community of trees stands tall, trunks reaching into the blue above, light filtering through leaves like perfect stained glass. (Unknown)

FINGER PAINT: LIKE WIDE-CARRIAGE PAPER: (PERSON) finger painting done on what looked like wide-carriage computer paper. (*PATRIOT GAMES* by Tom Clancy)

FIT: LIKE LONELY SHADOW: (PERSON) She fit into his loneliness like a shadow in a hollow. (Readers Digest *TOWARD MORE PICTURESQUE SPEECH*)

FLAMES DOTTING JUNGLE: LIKE ANGRY RED BOILS: (PERSON) he remembered Vietnam, remembered the bombing runs, remembered the flames dotting the jungle like angry red boils, playing tag with a Russian surface-to-air missile, or looking down at a VC bunker that had become the recipient of a five-hundred-pound bomb, he knew how to read the fiery dots and dashes of aerial warfare, as signs of success, failure, or danger. (*POWER PLAYS POLITIKA* by Tom Clancy and Martin Greenberg)

FLASH: LIKE BLINDING GLARE: (PERSON) His doctor had read his blood pressure and told him to take it easy. Sitting in his office two weeks later, he felt an electric flash in his head behind his eyes, a feeling like a blinding blue-white glare for a second, and then he couldn't read anymore. It wasn't that he couldn't see. He saw clearly enough, but the words on a page swam and ran together and squirmed like snakes, and he couldn't make out what they said. He knew he had had a stroke. (*THE WAYWARD BUS* by John Steinbeck)

FLASH: LIKE TEXAS STORM: (PERSON) She was like a Texas storm: sheet lightning with a sharp bright zigzag flashing across it. (*INSIGHT* Article by Jane Addams Allen)

FLAUNT: LIKE BANNER: (PERSON) ...swarthy, smiling face, the magnificent moustache that he flaunted like a banner. (*THE GUNS OF NAVORONE* by Alistair Maclean)

FLEE: LIKE SCHOOLKID: (PERSON) She had sworn she would never run away from anything again, but she had fled like a schoolkid. (*FINAL TARGET* by Iris Johansen)

FLIES SHOOT IN AND OUT: LIKE RUSHING STARS: (THING) At about ten o'clock in the morning the sun threw a bright dust-laden bar through one of the side windows, and in and out of the beam flies shot like rushing stars. (*OF MICE AND MEN* by John Steinbeck)

FLIES WHIP THROUGH SUNSHINE: LIKE SPARKS: (THING) The sun square was on the floor now, and the flies whipped through it like sparks. (

FLIP: LIKE TIDILY-WINK: TURTLE: THING:... over the grass at the roadside a land turtle crawled, turning aside for nothing, dragging his high-domed shell over the grass. His hard legs and yellow-nailed feet threshed slowly through the grass, not really walking, but boosting and dragging his shell along. The barley beads slid off his shell, and the clover burrs fell on him and rolled to the ground. His horny beak was partly open, and his fierce, humorous eyes, under brows like fingernails, stared straight ahead. He came over the grass leaving a beaten trail behind him, and the hill, which was the highway embankment, reared up ahead of him. For a moment he stopped, his head held high. He blinked and looked up and down. At last he started to climb the embankment. Front clawed feet reached forward but did not touch. The hind feet kicked his shell along, and it scraped on the grass, and on the gravel. As the embankment grew steeper and steeper, the more frantic were the efforts of the land turtle. Pushing hind legs strained and slipped, boosting the shell along, and the horny head protruded as far as the neck could stretch. Little by little the shell slid up the embankment until at last a parapet cut straight across its line of march, the shoulder of the road, a concrete wall four inches high. As though they worked independently the hind legs pushed the shell against the wall. The head upraised and peered over the wall to the broad smooth plain of cement. Now the hands raced on top of the wall, strained and lifted, and the shell came slowly up and rested its front end on the wall. For a moment the turtle rested. A red ant ran into the shell, into the soft skin inside the shell, and suddenly head and legs snapped in, and the armored tail clamped in sideways. The red ant was crushed between body and legs. And one head of wild oats was clamped into the shell by a front leg. For a long moment the turtle lay still, and then the neck crept out and the old humorous frowning eyes looked about and the legs and tail came out. The back legs went to work, straining like elephant legs, and the shell tipped to an angle so that the front legs could not reach the level cement plain. But higher and higher the hind legs boosted it, until at last the center of balance was reached, the front tipped down, the front legs scratched at the pavement, and it was up. But the head of wild oats was held by its stem around the front legs. - Now the going was easy, and all the legs worked, and the shell boosted along, waggling from side to side. ... now it hurried on, for the highway was burning hot. A light truck approached, and as it came near, the driver saw the turtle and swerved to hit it. His front wheel struck the edge of the shell, flipped the turtle like a tidily-wink, spun it like a coin, and rolled it off the highway. The truck went back to its course along the right side. Lying on its back, the turtle was tight in its shell for a long time. But at last its legs waved in the air, reaching for something to pull it over. Its front foot caught a piece of quartz and little by little the shell pulled over and flopped upright. The wild oat head fell out and three of the spearhead seeds stuck in the ground. And as the turtle crawled on down the embankment, its shell dragged dirt over the seeds. The turtle entered a dirt road and jerked itself along, drawing a wavy shallow trench in the dust with its shell. The old humorous eyes looked ahead, and the horny beak opened a little. His yellow toe nails slipped a fraction in the dust. *(THE GRAPES OF WRATH* by John Steinbeck)

    FLOAT: LIKE MIRAGE: (THING) The sky was a stormy blue, rain-washed but full of light; the green hills seemed to float in that brilliance like a mirage, reminiscent of a Tolkien illustration. Watery sunlight struck across the water making the rippling surface of the lake shimmer. (*CIRCLE OF FATE* by Charlotte Lamb)

FLOOD OVER: LIKE WATERS OF LAKE: (PERSON) Memories rushed back into her mind. All of it so raw, so real, flooding over her like the waters of the lake where she tried, and failed to end her own life. (*ABANDONED IN DEATH* by J. D. Robb)

FLOP: LIKE FISH ON LINE: (PERSON) Curley's fist was swinging when Lennie reached for it. The next minute Curley was flopped like a fish on a line, and his closed fist was lost in Lennie's big hand.. (*OF MICE AND MEN* by John Steinbeck)

FLOPPING: LIKE LANDED FISH: (PERSON) Not figuring the perp for a rabbit, the detective took him down and got a hole in the knee of her trousers for the effort. The perp was flopping around like a landed trout, and crying like a baby. (*MIDNIGHT SHADOWS* by Nora Roberts)

FLOW: LIKE RIVERS: STREET: (PLACE) This place seems so foreign now. The narrow streets flow like rivers, winding around hills and fields rather than cutting a Romanesque line through them. For the most part the lanes are one car wide and the corners blind, obscured behind the hawthorn hedgerow that has been growing unchecked through June and July, giddy with the sunshine and rain. I remember the white blooms and how they are so often over hung by spreading trees, darkening in the sunshine faster than I can tan. I recall the bird song and the gentleness of the sun, even in summer. Even the aroma takes me back to my misspent youth. But I've been gone too long and now this is like a half-forgotten dream. The good parts aren't as good as the memory and the bad parts are more frustrating. I'm just not used to it. As much as I want to savor the here and now I can't wait to board the plane for home; back to straight roads and summer heat that cooks your head. (Unknown)

THE METAPHORS OF LIKE

FLOW: LIKE RIVERS: TOWN: (PLACE) In that place I could be anyone, or perhaps no-one at all. The people flowed like rivers, never stopping for obstacles but swirling around them. On those wide avenues with wilted trees, their leaves curled and blackened in in the August heat, the buildings towered on each side. A hundred years ago I expect it was pretty, the golden light on the sandstone architecture, built in the days when curves and design weren't considered superfluous. Even the street-lamps were dreamt by an artist, built by an engineer following the teachings of a scientist. On days like this, crammed in with more bodies than I could count even in a photograph, I tilt my head to the sky. The empty blue gives me the strength just to walk at the pace of the crowd and bottle my claustrophobia inside my chest. (Unknown)

FLUFF FEST: LIKE UNSEEN FOR MONTHS: (THING) "It was a fluff fest like I've never seen for quite a few months there. And that seems to be transitioning a little bit away because perhaps they see the inevitable and they read the tea leaves, and again, they want that access to power. That, unfortunately, is such a big part of today's political process." (*RENEWED RIGHT.COM* 27Jul2023)

FLUTTER: LIKE SNOW IN GLASS GLOBE: (THING) ... the stuffing from the cushions fluttering about the room like the snow in her glass globe. (*RED STORM RISING* by Tom Clancy)

FLY ABOUT: LIKE SCATTERED BITS OF PAPER: THINK: (PERSON) Everything that had happened was flying about in her head like scattered bits of paper in a high wind. (*POWER PLAY* by Catherine Coulter)

FLY OVER: LIKE THEY COULD SENSE EVIL: FOREST: (PLACE) The woods were always quiet. It never heard the owls screeching, or the wolves howling. The place wasn't even close to what the myths had told the town people. Yet no one dared to walk through the woods, neither would they speak of it. The birds wouldn't fly over it, like they could even sense the evil in there. (Unknown)

FLYING CHAIN SHOT: LIKE HURTLING STAR: (THING) the dismantling shot in cylindrical canvas bags was a dozen six-foot lengths of iron chain, each joined to a single ring in the center. On discharge, they would fly like a hurtling star, effective to a range of 500 feet, cutting ropes and tearing canvas (and people) to shreds. (*THE CAPTAIN FROM CONNECTICUT* by C.S. Forester)

FOCUS: LIKE HIGH-DEF MOVIE: HARBOR: (PLACE) From the bow of the boat the harbor came into focus like a high-definition movie. Above the gulls swoop, crying in that repetitive way they do. The houses are identical in shape and size but no two are the same shade. They are yellow, lilac, blue, red, orange and every shade in between. Each one is not only a house but also a shop run by the folks that live above, selling ice-cream, meat, vegetables or fine leather goods. From the bright yellow lampposts hang the flags of European nations and in the town square there is a market. I can't see the fish from here, but I know from my many visits that they are there. Lying on those tables, silver scales to the sun, is the morning's catch. They are fresher than I can hope for back home, were the food has been frozen and breaded with seasoning and sugar some months before. The air here is fresher than in my dreams back in the city. One day I will come here and never leave. One day. (Unknown)

FOLD: LIKE CHEAP SUIT: (PERSON) The President folded like a cheap suit when he traded a notorious Russian arms dealer for a basketball player. (Online ' 12-14-2022)

FOLD: LIKE CHEAP SUIT: (PERSON) The Republican National Committee (RNC) folded like a cheap suit during the primary season by letting Democrats' hostile media allies host and moderate debates. (Tucker Carlson comment on *CONSERVATIVE UNDERGROUND NEWS* 12January2024)

FOLD: LIKE CHEAP TENT: (PERSON) The Iraqi Republican Guard soldier folded like a cheap tent. (Author)

THE METAPHORS OF LIKE 59

FOOL: LIKE TORPEDO: (PERSON) "She's like a torpedo heading straight for a target and not realizing she'll be blown up too." *(FINAL TARGET by Iris Johansen)*

FORGET: LIKE BOTTLE OF SANGRIA: (PERSON) he had forgotten it like a bottle of sangria left at the back of the refrigerator. (Author)

FORMATIONS LOOMED: LIKE PREHISTORIC BEASTS OUT OF PRIMEVAL MIST: (THING) The streaming snowflakes made the winter day appear to be a tapestry of millions of randomly arranged white threads. The false twilight of the storm brought a deep-gray gloom to the land three-quarters of an hour ahead of the real twilight. Gnarled, toothy rock formations and an occasional cottonwood loomed suddenly out of the murkiness like prehistoric beasts out of a primeval mist, never failing to startle. (Unknown)

FORMS: TREE-LIKE: (THING) Her artistic vocabulary included a series of ascending rounded stone or treelike forms, a jagged lightning bolt and a flat, wavy shape like a river. (*INSIGHT* Article by Jane Addams Allen)

FRAGMENTS: LIKE SCATTERED PIECES: FOREST: (PLACE) "In the forest the sky vanishes almost completely, only a few fragments of blue remain- like scattered pieces of an impossible jigsaw puzzle. The air is rich with the fragrance of leaves and loam, damp too. Even so many hours after the rains passed, the soil remains wet, slowly releasing its heavy fog. Outside is the noon daylight, the powerful rays of early summer, but in here everything is cool and the colors have the softness of that time just before twilight. The only movement is the occasional bird, startling in a bush or a squirrel dashing up a nearby trunk. The sound of running water in the brook has the same hypnotic quality as music. I want to stop just to drink in the sound. The huckleberries are mostly red, tart but with just the right amount of sweetness. I take in all the air my lungs will hold and expel it slowly. These hikes in the forest are like a trip out of my past, a visit to somewhere the measuring of time is done only by the rising and setting of the sun." (Unknown)

FREIGHT CAR: LIKE HEARSE: (THING) The Chrysler standing at the curb was more like a hearse than a freight car, black but not gleaming by reason of the droplets of rain and the greasy splash that rises from the highways. It carried frosted parking lights. *(THE WINTER OF OUR DISCONTENT* by John Steinbeck*)*

FRENCH: LIKE BILLIONAIRE PLAYBOY: (PERSON) His handsome face appeared on her computer screen—tanned, dark eyes, white teeth flashing, salt-and-pepper hair mussed from the salt spray, his Roman nose slightly pink from too much sun. His beard was beginning to gray a bit, but it only added to his charisma. He was so very French, like a billionaire playboy who'd parlayed his life into a fortune of holdings. (THE LAST SECOND by Catherine Coulter)

FRESH SNOW: LIKE BEING FIRST IN NEW WORLD: (THING) felt a curious excitement waling the new unmarked snow or frost; like being first in a new world, a deep, satisfying sense of discovery of something clean and new, unused, undirtied. *(THE WINTER OF OUR DISCONTENT* by John Steinbeck*)*

FURROWED: LIKE RUMPLED BROWN CORDUROY: HILLSIDE: (PLACE) a hillside furrowed like rumpled brown corduroy. (*RED STORM RISING* by Tom Clancy)

GAPE: ACTION: SEE: (PERSON) His first look at the Great Smoky Mountains had him gaping like a tourist in Times Square.. (*NIGHTWORK* by Nora Roberts)

GAS SMELL: LIKE DIESEL ON SNORKELING SUBMARINE: (THING) ... smelled like diesel in the control room on a snorkeling submarine. (*Unknown*)

GATHER: LIKE BLOOD CLOT: (PERSON) ... politicians coagulate in Washington like a blood clot. (*DAN BONGINO SHOW*, 17Aug2023)

THE METAPHORS OF LIKE   61

GESTURE: LIKE TRAFFIC COP: (PERSON) The President propped his right elbow on the table, formed a wide V with his thumb and forefinger, and leaned the bridge of his nose down into it. He simultaneously pushed his right palm out in the air like a traffic cop signaling the cars to a full stop. (*POWER PLAYS POLITIKA* by Tom Clancy and Martin Greenberg)

GIVE: LIKE CANDY: (PERSON) He gave copies out like candy. (*RECKONING* by Catherine Coulter)

GLARE: LIKE OUTRAGED DUCHESS: (PERSON) She deliberately glared at him like an outraged duchess being manhandled by the groom. (*LOVE UPON THE WIND* by Sally Stewart)

GLEAMING COLUMNS: LIKE TEETH: JERUSALEM: (PLACE) The Porch of Solomon faced them, the marble walls and Corinthian columns gleaming like teeth in a seven-foot mouth. Up the side of the great temple was the snowy stone wall, hung with a cluster of solid gold grapes four stories high. In the valley, the Golden Gate and the Fountain Gate slowly regurgitated the last of the temple pilgrims for the day. And from his place on the road, Joseph could look across the enclosed city and see Herod's palace on the far side, a little south of the place called Golgotha. (*THE DAY CHRIST WAS BORN* by Jim Bishop)

GLOW: LIKE JEWEL: (PERSON) the flower [in her hair] glowed there like a jewel against the pale cream of her nape. (*THE LIVING REED* by Pearl S. Buck)

GLOW: LIKE PINK FIRES: (THING) Under a transparent wash of gray lay the vibrant emerald of new-mown grass with the unfurled leaves of Hostas. Stretching through a bed of exuberant Astilbe were new tendrils of strawberry plants with blossoms that glowed like pink fires in the mist. (*OUT TO CANAAN* by Jan Karon)

GLOW: LIKE SEASHELLS: IRELAND: (PLACE) Roll after roll of green hills of Ireland shimmered under sunlight that glowed like the inside of seashells and spread back and back into the shadows of dark mountains. The hulk of them rambled against a sky layered with smoky clouds and pearly light that belonged in paintings rather than reality. *(JEWELS OF THE SUN by Nora Roberts)*

GLOWING LIGHT: LIKE INSIDE OF PEARL: (THING) It was a perfect day for a walk. The light glowed like the inside of a pearl. Luminous, with a slight sheen of damp. One could see, over the hills and fields rolling toward the mountains, a thin and silvery curtain that was certainly a line of rain. Sunlight poured through the curtain in beams and ripples, liquid gold through liquid silver. It was the kind of day that begged for rainbows. *(JEWELS OF THE SUN by Nora Roberts)*

GRAVEYARD: LOOKED LIKE RESTING PLACE OF GENERATIONS: CHURCH: (PLACE) The ancient church on the hill had to have been built centuries ago, and the graveyard stretching behind it, looked like the resting place of generations of villagers. The church building itself had no windows, and the stone steps led up to massive, splintered oak doors. *(FINAL TARGET by Iris Johansen)*

GREEN VALLEY: LIKE SPRIG OF PARSLEY IN BOWL (PERSON) They walked down out of the mountains into the lush green valley, which appeared to lie like a sprig of parsley in the bottom of a bowl. (*THE DAY CHRIST DIED* by Jim Bishop)

GRIN: LIKE SURVEYING CRIPPLED ANTELOPE: (PERSON) He grinned like a lion surveying a herd of crippled antelope. (*PATRIOT GAMES* by Tom Clancy)

GRIP: LIKE GIANT STEEL PINCERS: (PERSON) gasped in pain as Andrea's fingers caught his arm like giant steel pincers. (Unknown)

GRIP: LIKE VISE: (PERSON) "I have a voice, he said, "a young voice. Will you give me your hand, my kind, young friend, and lead me in?" I held out my hand, and the horrible, soft-spoken, eyeless creature gripped it in a moment, like a vise. I was so much startled that I struggled to withdraw; but the blind man pulled me close up to him with a single action of his arm. "Now boy, he sneered, "take me in to the captain. "Come, now, march. Lead me straight up to him, and when

I'm in view, cry out. 'Here's a friend for you, Bill.' If you don't, I'll do this," and he gave me a twitch that I thought would have made me faint. (*TREASURE ISLAND* by Robert Louis Stevenson)

GRIZZLED: LIKE DOG: (PERSON) He was clean-shaven, but not since yesterday, and along the corners of his chin and on his neck the coming whiskers were grizzled and white like those of an old Airedale. This was the more apparent because the rest of his beard was so intensely black. (THE WAYWARD BUS by John Steinbeck)

GROW ALONG SAND: LIKE BRAMBLES: LIKE OAK: WOODS: (PLACE) He came to a long thicket of oak-like trees—live, or evergreen oaks. I heard afterward they should be called—which grew along the sand like brambles, the boughs curiously twisted, the foliage compact, like thatch. The thicket stretched down from the top of one of the sandy knolls, spreading and growing taller as it went, until it reached the margin of the broad, reedy fen, through which the nearest of the little rivers soaked its way into the anchorage. The marsh was steaming in the strong sun, and the outline of the Spyglass trembled through the haze. (*TREASURE ISLAND* by Robert Louis Stevenson)

GROW WITH LAYERS: LIKE ONION: (THING) Like an onion, it grew larger as more coats were added to its thickness. The layers of new skin were then slowly unpeeled to reveal the treasure at the core. (Unknown)

GROW: LIKE MOLD: He'll grow on you … like mold. (*MIDNIGHT SHADOWS* by Nora Roberts)

GROW: LIKE WEED: (PERSON) … grew like a weed in a fertilized garden. (Author)

HAIR HANGING: LIKE SAUSAGES: GIRL: (PERSON) Both men glanced up, for the rectangle of sunshine in the doorway was cut off. A girl was standing there looking in. She had full, rouged lips and wide-spaced eyes, heavily made up. Her fingernails were red. Her hair hung in little rolled clusters, like sausages. She wore a cotton house dress and red mules, on the insteps of which were little bouquets of red ostrich feathers.. (*OF MICE AND MEN* by John Steinbeck)

HAIR: LIKE FLASHING SIGN: (PERSON) Some redheads with green eyes are so stunning that seeing one can stop you like a flashing "don't walk sign." (*BRIT-AM* 3319)

HAIR: LIKE HORSE MANE: (PERSON) the wind blowing her pale hair behind her like the mane of a wild horse and her cloak billowing, white as the moon overhead. (*JEWELS OF THE SUN by Nora Roberts*)

HAIR: LIKE POODLE: (PERSON) She had a poodle-like hairdo. (Author)

HAIR: LIKE PRINCESS: (PERSON) her glossy black hair framing her exquisite face, like a princess with black-framed glasses and intelligent eyes. She wore diamonds in her ears and on her wrist, and her wedding ring sparkled and gleamed in the bright lights. (*RECKONING* by Catherine Coulter)

HANDSOME: MALE: RIDER: (PERSON) He dismounted and was partly drunk; that was not the striking thing about him. He looked and breathed the very spirit of the range at its wildest. He was tall, lean and lithe, with a handsome red face, like a devil's eyes, hot as blue flame, and yellow hair that curled scraggily from under a dusty black sombrero. He had just been clean-shaved. Drops of blood and sweat stood out like beads on his lean jowls and curved lips. A gun swung below his hip. (*SUNSET PASS* by Zane Grey)

HANG CLOTHES: LIKE MINDLESS PROCESS: (PERSON) It seemed like a mindless and thereby soul-soothing process. The woman took pegs from the pocket of her apron, clamped them in her mouth as she bent to take a pillowcase from the basket. She snapped it briskly, and then clamped it to the line. The next item was dealt with in the same way and shared the second peg. (*JEWELS OF THE SUN* by Nora Roberts)

THE METAPHORS OF LIKE

HANG OVER: LIKE GREAT SORROW: (THING) ... and the sweet smell is a great sorrow on the land. ... Men who have created new fruits in the world cannot create a system whereby their fruits may be eaten by the hungry people. And the failure hangs over the State like a great sorrow. ... a sorrow here that weeping cannot symbolize. There is a failure here that topples all their success. ... because a profit cannot be taken from the fruit. *(THE GRAPES OF WRATH by John Steinbeck)*

HANG: LIKE GOLDEN FRUIT: LAND: (PLACE) ... The peninsula hung like a golden fruit before the longing eyes of the surrounding nations, proud China, vast Russia, and Japan. *(JEWELS OF THE SUN by Nora Roberts)*

HANG: LIKE THUNDER CLOUD: (PERSON) Mutiny hung over them like a thunder cloud. *(TREASURE ISLAND by Robert Louis Stevenson)*

HANGING DUST: LIKE FOG: (THING) The people knew it would take a long time for the dust to settle out of the air. In the morning the dust hung like fog, and the sun was as red as ripe new blood. All day the dust sifted down from the sky, and the next day it sifted down. An even blanket covered the earth. It settled on the corn, piled up on the tops of fence posts, piled up on the wires; it settled on roofs, blanketed the weeds and trees. *(THE GRAPES OF WRATH by John Steinbeck)*

HANGING ON: LIKE TATTERED REMAINS OF XYLOPHONE: (THING) missing arches in the bridge washed out by the raging river; steel rails sagging across the open gap and a few wooden ties hanging on like the tattered remains of a giant xylophone. *(WATCHING FOR THE WIND by James G. Edinger)*

HAPPY: ACTION: (PERSON) like a couple of kids on an endless spring break. *(HEAVEN AND EARTH by Nora Roberts)*

HAT: LOOKED LIKE DRUNKEN ADMIRAL: (THING) I put the hat on the newel post of the banister, and it looked like a drunken admiral if there is such a thing. (*THE WINTER OF OUR DISCONTENT* by John Steinbeck)

HATBOX SUPPORT: LIKE UPSIDE-DOWN PORRIDGE BOWL: (PERSON) The leather hatbox was open on the floor. It had a support made of velvet-covered cardboard like an upside-down porridge bowl. (*THE WINTER OF OUR DISCONTENT* by John Steinbeck)

HEAD HELD UP: LIKE LITTLE PERISCOPE: (THING) A water snake slipped along on the pool, its head held up like a little periscope. (*OF MICE AND MEN* by John Steinbeck)

HEADS TURN TOGETHER: LIKE WATCHING HORSE RACE: (PERSON) You could see their heads turn [together], like watching a horse race. (*THE WAYWARD BUS* by John Steinbeck)

HEARING: LIKE TRYING TO GRAB CLOUD: (PERSON) Hearing that distant low sound was like trying to grab for a cloud of smoke. It was only when she didn't try to—but she had to grab it! (*THE CARDINAL OF THE KREMLIN* by Tom Clancy)

HEART BEAT FIERCELY: LIKE THAT SINCE BIKERS CAME TO TOWN: STREET: (PLACE) I have walked these streets my whole life, I know them just the same as if they were etched in my head with a sharp knife, scored in deep like some strange work of art. These are the streets I grew up on and for the most part I'm calm here, at home, on the down low with a steady heartbeat. Not tonight though. Tonight my heart wants out of my chest. It wants to beat free of its cage. It pounds like it's going to crack a rib. My senses are on high alert. Every color is brighter, every noise louder, every stranger a cause to make my heart beat more fiercely still. It's been like that since the bikers came to town, marking out their turf like a wolf pack. I don't even deal drugs but they mean to dominate everyone regardless. They've got Kenny dealing for them already, there goes his grades, and there goes his life. So now the streets that were my salvation spike my adrenaline as good as a shot to the arm. (Unknown)

HEAT COVERED AREA: LIKE EVIL SPELL: (THING) His car didn't have air conditioning. The drive home was complicated by all the people heading to the beach for the weekend, anything to get away from the heat that had covered the area like an evil spell for two weeks. (*PATRIOT GAMES* by Tom Clancy)

HEAT WAVES RISE: LIKE BATTALIONS OF GHOSTLY BEINGS: (THING) The hot, dry day caused heat waves to rise in columns like battalions of ghostly beings. (Unknown)

HEAT: EYES: LIKE STOVE: (PERSON) His eyes heated up like a stove when his interest was aroused. (*THE WAYWARD BUS* by John Steinbeck)

HEAVE: LIKE THE SEA DURING EARTHQUAKE: (THING) The earthquake caused the land to heave like the sea. (*TREASURE ISLAND* by Robert Louis Stevenson)

HEAVY ROSEBUSHES: LIKE CORSET NO LONGER CONCEALING STOMACH: (THING) The gathering brass of dawn showed rosebushes heavy with middle-aged blooms, like women whose corseting no longer conceals a thickening stomach, no matter how pretty their legs may remain. (*THE WINTER OF OUR DISCONTENT* by John Steinbeck)

HELPLESS: LIKE ON RUNAWAY TRAIN: (PERSON) It was like being on a runaway train. I knew what was coming, but there wasn't anything I could do about it. (*FINAL TARGET* by Iris Johansen)

HIDDEN: LIKE ANCHOR: (PERSON) His idea of right and wrong was his means of gauging his actions and those of others. It served as an anchor for his soul and, like an anchor it was hidden far below the visible surface. (*THE HUNT FOR RED OCTOBER by Tom Clancy*)

HIKE: LIKE TRIP OUT OF PAST: FOREST: (PLACE) "In the forest the sky vanishes almost completely, only a few fragments of blue remain- like scattered pieces of an impossible jigsaw puzzle. The air is rich with the fragrance of leaves and loam, damp too. Even so many hours after the rains passed, the soil remains wet, slowly releasing its heavy fog. Outside is the noon daylight, the powerful rays of early summer, but in here everything is cool and the colors have the softness of that time just before twilight. The only movement is the occasional bird, startling in a bush or a squirrel dashing up a nearby trunk. The sound of running water in the brook has the same hypnotic quality as music. I want to stop just to drink in the sound. The huckleberries are mostly red, tart but with just the right amount of sweetness. I take in all the air my lungs will hold and expel it slowly. These hikes in the forest are like a trip out of my past, a visit to somewhere the measuring of time is done only by the rising and setting of the sun." (Unknown)

HISS: ACTION: LAUGH: (PERSON) Her laughter shot out like bolts, cracked the black bowl of the sky. A torrent of dark rain fell and hissed on the sand like acid. (*HEAVEN AND EARTH* by Nora Roberts)

HISSING SOUND: LIKE MOVING STREAM: (THING) The low hiss of their whispering sounded continuously in my ear like a moving stream. (*TREASURE ISLAND* by Robert Louis Stevenson)

HIT: LIKE A CLUB: (PLACE) As soon as he got inside the CIA building, the ambience of spook central hit him like a club. He saw eight security officers, all in civilian clothes now, their jackets unbuttoned to suggest the presence of side arms. What they really carried was radios, but Jack was sure that men with guns were only a few feet away. The walls had cameras that fed into some central monitoring room—Ryan didn't know where that was; in fact, the only parts of the building he actually knew were the path to his cubbyhole office, from there to the men's room, and the route to the cafeteria. There was something about this place that made him instantly paranoid. (*PATRIOT GAMES* by Tom Clancy)

HOARD: LIKE SCROOGE MCDUCK: (PERSON) sitting on his money like Scrooge McDuck. (*HEARTLAND* by Bethany Campbell)

HOLD: LIKE BEAR TRAP: (PERSON) The criminal squirmed and snapped in his own cold-blooded way, but the cop had a grip like a bear trap and didn't let go. (*MIDNIGHT SHADOWS* by Nora Roberts)

HOP: LIKE BIRD: (PERSON) A man came out of a side room, and at a glance, I was sure he must be Long John. His left leg was cut off close by the hip, and under the left shoulder he carried a crutch, which he managed with wonderful dexterity, hopping about upon it like a bird. He was very tall and strong, with a face as big as a ham—plain and pale, but intelligent and smiling. Indeed, he seemed in the most cheerful spirits, whistling as he moved about among the tables with a merry word or a slap on the shoulder for the more favored of his guests. (*TREASURE ISLAND* by Robert Louis Stevenson)

HOPE: LIKE SPRING: (THING) Hope feels like spring, like something new and better is on the horizon. (*DISCOVERING DANIEL* by Amir Tsarfati)

HORNY KNEES: LIKE CAMEL: (PERSON) The little man who was standing close to one of the stone columns with his eyes on Jesus most of the time was called James of Alphaeus (not be confused with the brother of Jesus), and someday he would be called other things, like James the Lesser and James the Just. This man was shy to the point of pain. When he spoke, it was his custom to whisper. He was the shortest of the group. His father was Alphaeus; his mother was reputed to be a woman named Mary who, in turn, was said to be a sister to the Mother of Jesus. James of Alphaeus was always addressed by Jesus as "my brother," And this James loved him dearly, but had difficulty believing that Jesus was the Messiah. He was older than Jesus and had known him from infancy. All of them were strict Jews, but James of Alphaeus carried the law beyond strictness to the point of fanaticism. He never touched wine of liquor or meat (except where Scripture enjoined him to); would not anoint his hair or take a bath. He prayed so often on his knees that they became "horny like those of a camel." He had seen his "cousin" perform many works of wonder in the past two years, but James, a paragon of intellectual honesty, found himself admitting, on occasion, that Jesus was indeed the Messiah, and then, a few days or a few weeks later, found himself wavering in his belief. (THE DAY CHRIST DIED by Jim Bishop)

HOT AIR CLARITY: LIKE LOOKING THROUGH SHIMMERING MIRAGE: (THING) The hot air rising off the desert in the early morning was disturbed enough to ruin the clarity of the satellite image. But they could make out six men lined up on a firing line. It was like looking through a shimmering mirage on a flat highway. (*PATRIOT GAMES* by Tom Clancy)

HOUSE SMELL: LIKE OLD GUY'S HOUSE: (THING) When the door opened, the place smelled like an old guy's house. (*POWER PLAY* by Catherine Coulter)

HOUSE: LOOKED LIKE FAVORITE RESIDENCE OF BATS: (PLACE) The whole place was derelict. The woodshed was huge, but rickety, and had clearly not been used for years. The implement sheds were slowly sinking into the long grass, and the house looked like a favorite residence of bats. (*COUNTRY OF THE HEART* by Robyn Donald)

HOUSES ON SLOPE: LIKE CUBES OF SUGAR: (PERSON) Peabody looked over at Nevis, at the white houses of Charlestown broadcast over the green slopes like cubes of sugar. (*THE CAPTAIN FROM CONNECTICUT* by C.S. Forester)

HOVER: LIKE HELICOPTER: (PERSON) His mother hovered over him like a helicopter. (Reader's Digest *TOWARD MORE PICTURESQUE SPEECH*)

HULL SOUND: DISLIKED BY SUBMARINER: (THING) The lash of the sonar waves had resounded through the hull. It was not a sound a submariner likes to hear. (Tom Clancy, *THE HUNT FOR RED OCTOBER*)

HUM: LIKE MOAN OF PLEASURE AND LONGING: (THING) She had the magic talisman mound of stone in her hands, caressing it with her fingers, petting it as though it were alive. She pressed it against her unformed breast, placed it on her cheek below her ear, nuzzled it like a suckling puppy, and she hummed a low song like a moan of pleasure and of longing. It was mother, lover, and child, in her hands. *(THE WINTER OF OUR DISCONTENT* by John Steinbeck*)*

HUNG OVER: LIKE SWORD OF DAMOCLES: (PERSON) His disease hung over him like the sword of Damocles, always in the back of his mind, influencing every word he spoke and every action he took. *(POWER PLAY* by Catherine Coulter*)*

HUNG: LIKE AFTERTHOUGHTS: AIRCRAFT: (THING) Nearly all tactical aircraft had pleasing lines conferred on them by the need in combat for speed and maneuverability. Not the Hog, which was perhaps the ugliest bird ever built for the U.S. Air Force. Her twin turbofan engines hung like afterthoughts at the twin-rudder tail, itself a throwback to the thirties. Her slab-like wings had not a whit of sweepback and were bent in the middle to accommodate the clumsy landing gear. The undersides of the wings were studded with many hard points so ordnance could be carried, and the fuselage was built around the aircraft's primary weapon, the GAU-8 thirty-millimeter rotary cannon designed specifically to smash Soviet tanks. *(THE HUNT FOR RED OCTOBER by* Tom Clancy*)*

HUNG: LIKE MARIONETTE ON STICK: (PERSON) He leaned out over the cliff, straddling the strong branch, and tied the thick leather thong to it. Then he took the other end of the string and tied it securely around his neck. He made several knots behind his ear, and then slowly, carefully, he crept out on the branch. The little man clung to the wood with both hands for a moment. His eyes looked directly up into the sun, and he whimpered like a child who is afraid that something is going to hurt. Then he released one hand, and the other. He dropped a few feet and, in the morning sun, swung back and forth like a lazy pendulum. The branch creaked as he swung. After a few seconds, he reached up to the leather thong and dried to grasp it and lift himself up. His mouth opened and contorted, but no sound came.

The legs convulsed and drew themselves up, almost to his chest. He made one more attempt to pull himself up, then his hands fell back and settled by his side and he swung back and forth in a wide arc. He hung like a marionette on a stick and moved no more. (*THE DAY CHRIST DIED* by Jim Bishop)

HUNG: LIKE THUNDER CLOUD: (THING) Mutiny hung over them like a thunder cloud. (*TREASURE ISLAND* by Robert Louis Stevenson)

HUNG: LIKE VEIL UNDER INVISIBLE CEILING: Blue smoke was curling out from the chimneys of many houses and hung, like a veil under an invisible ceiling over the city. (*THE DAY CHRIST DIED* by Jim Bishop)

HUNG: LIKE VEIL: HOUSE: (PLACE) Blue smoke curled from many homes and hung, like a veil under an invisible ceiling. (*THE DAY CHRIST DIED* by Jim Bishop)

HURT: LIKE THROWING SNOWBALL: (PERSON) Relating to those families was going to hurt her big time. But she was determined. In the end he concluded that stopping her would be like throwing a snowball at an avalanche. (*QUINN* by Iris Johansen)

IDEA POPPING UP: LIKE BUBBLES IN SODA POP: (THING) Ideas kept popping up like bubbles in soda pop. *(THE GRAPES OF WRATH* by John Steinbeck*)*

IDEAS CRACKLING: LIKE LIGHTNING: (THING) ideas were crackling across the room like lightning. (*PATRIOT GAMES* by Tom Clancy)

IMAGINE LEAVES: LIKE QUILT OVER GROUND: (THING) The falling leaves flutter down, sparse in the cool mid-autumn air. In other places perhaps they are a feast of colors - enough to feed the soul as well as the eyes. I've read about leaves like that, I've imagined them like a garish quilt over the ground. Perhaps if I saw them I'd be poetical too, but these leaves are all brown. The only difference between now and winter is the crunch underfoot and soon even that will be dampened by the rains. (Unknown)

IMPOSSIBLE: LIKE NAILING JELL-O TO TREE: (THING) like trying to nail Jell-O to a tree. (Unknown)

INSINCERE: LIKE CICADAS: (PERSON) Like cicadas, these career political hacks come out during election years making loud promises while trying to cover up their previous failures with a ton of lies. (Online posting June 7, 2024)

INSINCERE: LIKE MACKEREL: (PERSON) ... like a Mackerel in the moonlight—it shined but it still stunk. (Unknown)

INTERRELATED: LIKE PUZZLE: (PERSON) Several things were interrelated like some kind of three-dimensional crossword puzzle. He didn't know the number of blanks, and he didn't have any of the clues to the words, but he did know roughly the way they fit together. (*PATRIOT GAMES* by Tom Clancy)

INTERTWINED: LIKE BOWL OF SPAGHETTI: (THING) the political career of President Joe Biden and the business of the Biden family were intricately intertwined, much like a bowl of spaghetti. (*CONSEERVATIVE ADVOCACY* newsletter 8Dec2023)

INVADE: LIKE ALIENS: (PERSON) From the moment he walked in, he felt completely out of his element. From the hairstyles to the clothes to the exaggerated mannerisms, these people were just ... weird. It's like they were aliens who had invaded from planet Loud. (*OPERATION JOKTAN* by Amir Tsarfati and Steve Yohn)

JERK: LIKE BESERK ROLLER COASTER: (THING) Worst of all, they were flying through a storm at 5,000 feet, and the COD (plane) was jerking up and down in hundred-foot gulps like a berserk roller coaster. (*THE HUNT FOR RED OCTOBER* by Tom Clancy)

JINGLING SOUND: LIKE SMALL BELLS RATTLING: (THING) He heard the sound of jingling keys, like small bells rattling to the measured tread of someone walking. (*PATRIOT GAMES* by Tom Clancy)

JOIN: LIKE HIMSELF: (PERSON) He was a businessman, president of a medium-sized corporation, and he was never alone. His business was conducted by groups of men who worked alike, thought alike, and even looked alike. His lunches were with men like himself who joined together in clubs so that no foreign element or idea could enter. His religious life was again his lodge and his church, both of which were screened and protected. One night a week he played poker with men so exactly like himself that the game was fairly even, and from this fact his group was convinced that they were very fine poker players. Wherever he went he was not one man but a unit in a corporation, a unit in a club, in a lodge, in a church, in a political party. His thoughts and ideas were never subjected to criticism since he willingly associated only with people like himself. He read a newspaper written by and for his group. He books that came into his house were chosen by a committee which deleted material that might irritate him. He hated foreign countries and foreigners because it was difficult to find his counterpart in them. He did not want to stand out from his group. He would like to have risen to the top of it and be admired by it, but it would not occur to him to leave it. (*THE WAYWARD BUS* by John Steinbeck)

JUMP: LIKE MANUFACTORY: (THING) The Hispaniola was rolling scuppers under in the ocean swell. The booms were tearing at the blocks, the rudder was banging to and fro, and the whole ship creaking, groaning, and jumping like a manufactory. The ship was being rolled about like a bottle. (*TREASURE ISLAND* by Robert Louis Stevenson)

JUMP: LIKE SCARED GRASSHOPPER: (PERSON) He jumped like a scared grasshopper. (Author)

KICK: LIKE STEER: (PERSON) The boy carrying the bag of nuts groaned and complained about the weight until; his friend said, "You'd be kicking like a steer if you didn't have to carry [nuts], and now you're sore because you have enough to last all winter." (*THE RADIO BOYS AT MOUNTAIN PASS* by Allen Chapman)

KNOCK DOWN: LIKE POLE-AXED COW: (PERSON) ... went down like a pole-axed cow. (*THE WINTER OF OUR DISCONTENT* by John Steinbeck)

KNOCKED OFF FEET: LIKE RAG DOLL: (PERSON) The vest stopped the bullet, but its impact hurt. She rubbed a hand between her breasts, acknowledging the breathless pain. It made a softball-size bruise and knocked her off her feet, tossing her like a rag doll. (*MIDNIGHT SHADOWS* by Nora Roberts)

LASER ON SATELLITE: LOOKED LIKE DIPPED IN MOLTEN STEEL: (THING) The laser made the satellite look like it was dipped in a ladle of molten steel. What had been flat surfaces were now rippled from the intense heat that was still radiating away. The solar cells arrayed on the body of the satellite—which were designed to absorb light energy—appeared to be burned off entirely. On closer inspection, the entire satellite body was distorted from the energy that had blasted it. (*THE CARDINAL OF THE KREMLIN* by Tom Clancy)

LASH: ACTION: STAND: (PERSON) She stood, arms out-flung in the tempest she had conjured. Her hair flew free and wild, dark ribbons that lashed at the night like whips. (*HEAVEN AND EARTH* by Nora Roberts)

LASH: LIKE GIANT COCOON: (PERSON) The drunken sailors were being lashed into their hammocks like giant cocoons that could neither hurt themselves nor anyone else. (*THE CAPTAIN FROM CONNECTICUT* by C.S. Forester)

LAUGH SOUND: LIKE GOLDEN GLORY: (THING) I heard ... laugh like golden glory. *(THE WINTER OF OUR DISCONTENT* by John Steinbeck*)*

LAUGH: LIKE CHILDREN: (PERSON) laughing like a couple of children. (*CIRCLE OF FATE* by Charlotte Lamb)

LAUGH: LIKE FLASH OF SUNLIGHT: (PERSON) warmth hovered in the air between them; the possibility of shared laughter was like the flash of sunlight on water. (Unknown)

LAUGH: LIKE LOONS: (PERSON) The twins enjoyed their regular nine hours and were raring to go at six thirty that morning. Molly found them already on their parent's bed talking twin talk a thousand miles an hour, hopping up and down, laughing like loons. (*RECKONING* by Catherine Coulter)

LAUGH: LIKE TEENAGER: (PERSON) she acted and moved like a teenager, either crashing about noisily or laughing like a hyena over nothing. (*CIRCLE OF FATE* by Charlotte Lamb)

LAY FLAT: LIKE FUR: HEAD: (PERSON) He raised his head, and his bristled chin showed in the light and his stringy neck where the whiskers lay flat like fur. (*THE GRAPES OF WRATH* by John Steinbeck)

LEAP FORWARD: LIKE SPURRED HORSE: (THING) The pilot pushed the throttles to the stops and punched in the afterburners. The fighter leaped forward like a spurred horse, accelerating through Mach 1 in seconds. (*RED STORM RISING* by Tom Clancy)

LEAP: LIKE WILD STAG: (PERSON) When she woke it was full dark, and the little peat fire had burned down to tiny ruby lights. She stared at them, her eyes bleary with sleep, her heart leaping like a wild stag in her throat as she mistook the embers for watching eyes. (*JEWELS OF THE SUN* by Nora Roberts)

LEAVES: LIKE QUILT: FOREST: (PLACE) The falling leaves flutter down, sparse in the cool mid-autumn air. In other places perhaps they are a feast of colors - enough to feed the soul as well as the eyes. I've read about leaves like that, I've imagined them like a garish quilt over the ground. Perhaps if I saw them I'd be poetical too, but these leaves are all brown. The only difference between now and winter is the crunch underfoot and soon even that will be dampened by the rains. (Unknown)

LENGTHEN: LIKE LITTLE GREEN BIRD'S EGGS: (THING) The prunes lengthen like little green bird's eggs, and the limbs sag down against the crutches under the weight. The year is heavy with produce. *(THE GRAPES OF WRATH* by John Steinbeck*)*

LID FLY UP: LIKE WAVING FLAG: (THING) He reached inside for the car's trunk-lid release button. The button clicked and the trunk lid flew up, waving like a flag in the woods. The sun shone through the trees of the thick woods and glinted off that trunk lid. *(AGENT TO THE RESCUE* by Lisa Childs*)*

LIFT: LIKE SACK OF COAL: (PERSON) ... hauled up like a sack of coals. (Unknown)

LIGHT SEEPING IN: LIKE FLOOD WATER: (THING) To the east the sky grew pink. All of a sudden the mountains of the island changed from vague shadowy slopes to sharp hard outlines which might have been cut from black paper and laid against the brightness, Round the sides of the outline the light came seeping like flood water round an obstruction. (*THE CAPTAIN FROM CONNECTICUT* by C.S. Forester)

LIGHT UP: LIKE CANDLE: (PERSON) Her face lit up like a candle. (*ABANDONED IN DEATH* by J. D. Robb)

LIGHT UP: LIKE FIREFLY: (PERSON) Her face lit up like a firefly. (*Author*)

LIKE FORCE OF NATURE: (PERSON) He was like a force of nature—unconquerable, proud, untamed and untamable. (*HEARTLAND* by Bethany Campbell)

LIKE LOOK OF: ACTION: (PERSON) He liked the look of the hills, a roll he'd only seen in pictures or movies. He imagined them summer green, rising and falling, behind fields of grazing horses. (*NIGHTWORK* by Nora Roberts)

LIKE LOOK OF: STORE: (PLACE) He liked the look of the store even more on the inside. The cheerful fire in a stone hearth, the big checkout counter carved with moons and stars. Seventeenth century, he decided, and suitable for a museum. (*HEAVEN AND EARTH* by Nora Roberts)

LIKE WATER-DUST: (THING) It was like water-dust at the foot of the falls. (Unknown)

LIKE: SOUND: OCEAN: (THING) He had always liked the sound of the sea, especially at night when it seemed to fill the world. (*HEAVEN AND EARTH* by Nora Roberts)

LIKED BEST: ACTION: THINK: (PERSON) Alone was another thing she liked best. There was a great deal to think about. Some of which she preferred not to, so she tucked those annoyances and problems away for now.. (*HEAVEN AND EARTH* by Nora Roberts)

LIKED LOOKING AT: WOMAN: (PERSON) her hair was all over her head in wild tangles, her face clean of makeup. He had to admit he really liked looking at her. (*POWER PLAY* by Catherine Coulter)

LINE FLOOR: LIKE BREADCRUMBS: HALLWAY: (PLACE) ... stuff strewn around the hallway. Empty beer cans, liquor bottles and fast-food bags lined the floor like breadcrumbs leading further down the hall. (Unknown)

LINE UP: LIKE ADVANCE GUARD: ROAD: (PLACE) As the seasons came and went the avenue changed its color palate. In the fall it was all about red, the winter brought brown and white, while the warmer months were simply green with splashes of summer blooms. The trees were lined up like an advance guard, Jenny liked that. She imagined they were soldiers frozen in time, their boughs at the ready, but then she loved Tolkien more than most. Rain or shine she let her fingers brush against their gnarled trunks on the way to her morning bus; there was something about the feel, something of the earth. But no matter the time of year the traffic stayed the same, a procession of cars with drivers focusing only on their destination rather than the journey. Jenny wondered if they even noticed the leafy guardians about them, ever raised their eyes from the weary tarmac. (Unknown)

LINED UP: LIKE LADIES: COTTAGE: PLACE:... cottages were pretty, lined up like ladies with flowers at their feet. *(JEWELS OF THE SUN by Nora Roberts)*

LIPS: LIKE DRAWN ZIPPERS: (PERSON) ... lips were like drawn zippers. (Readers Digest *TOWARD MORE PICTURESQUE SPEECH*)

LIVING ROOM SMELLED: LIKE FADED VIOLETS: (THING) He walked the old man to his couch in a living room that smelled like faded violets. (*POWER PLAY* by Catherine Coulter)

LOAD CHEEKS: LIKE SACKS: (PERSON) Squirrels bank ten times as many hickory nuts as they can ever use. The pocket gopher, with a stomach full to bursting, still loads his cheeks like sacks. And how much of the honey, the clever bees collect do the clever bees actually eat? *Source: THE WINTER OF OUR DISCONTENT by John Steinbeck)*

LOOK LIKE: ACTION: LAUGH: (PERSON) He walked in to see [them] at the kitchen table laughing. Mag's short skullcap of hair blasted a sapphire blue. But his mother's short new growth in bubblegum pink knocked him back. Harry said, "I think you look like Easter eggs. If they had them on Mars." That brought on more insane laughter. (*NIGHTWORK* by Nora Roberts)

LOOKED LIKE 19TH CENTURY SHRINKING VIOLET: (PERSON) She looked like a 19th century shrinking violet. (Author)

LOOKED LIKE DIPPED IN SUGAR: MOUNTAINS: (PLACE) ... light snow and cold air made the mountains look like they were dipped in sugar. (*Unknown*)

LOOKED LIKE EDGE OF SPRAWLING CORNFIELD: TOWN: (PLACE) Interstate 80 runs by Dixon, California but not through it. The traffic on I-80 streams between San Francisco and Sacramento shooting by the town leaving travelers unaware that a town is out there. Only a cattle auction yard and restaurant are visible to passing motorists. Otherwise, Dixon looks like the edge of a sprawling cornfield. (*ADVENTURE ROAD* magazine Sep-Oct 1987)

LOOKED LIKE FAIRY REALM: MISTY MAINLAND: (PLACE) The mainland looked like a fairy realm glimpsed through the mists of fantasy, unreal, with its bulk brooded over by a mountain blue as grapes in the summer haze. (*COUNTRY OF THE HEART* by Robyn Donald)

LOOKED LIKE GIANT SNAKE: WOUND ALONG HIGHWAY: CARS: (PLACE) ... the cars looked like a giant snake as they wound their way along the highway. *(FINAL TARGET* by Iris Johansen*)*

LOOKED LIKE GREW OUT OF GROUND: FAÇADE: (PLACE) The ledge was more like a rocky outcrop, rustic and rough. It was in keeping with the building, only three years old but made to look as if it were ancient. The rocks had been trucked in from some quarry up north and the builders had to consult with old-fashioned brick layers to get the rock facade right. It was all steel and concrete underneath of course, but from out here it looked like it just grew right out of the ground. On the ledge should have been pigeons, peering down in the way they do, looking for pedestrians dropping fragments of their breakfasts. But in the frosted dawn-light the ledge is layered with roses, red, white and pink. It could be a romantic gesture from some eccentric billionaire, but it isn't. It's one rose for day of the empresses' life... (Unknown)

LOOKED LIKE SCARED RELIC OF WAR: TOWN: (PLACE) The small town was long and littered with battered gas stations and multitudes of peeling billboards. The town was active in the 30s before the interstate came through and bypassed whole area of America. This town looked like the scarred relic of a war for development and perceived progress. The town's fortunes followed a roller coaster path. Bustling and lively with the gold mines nearby, the town's economy sank when the mines closed and highways and railroad lines skirted the community. (*ADVENTURE ROAD* magazine Sep-Oct 1987)

LOOKED LIKE TEMPLE: (PLACE) Looking like an awesome contemporary Greek temple, the Visitor Center is set into the reservation hillside and points visitors toward the sites. (*ADVENTURE ROAD* magazine, Sep/Oct 1987)

LOOKED LIKE UNFINISHED PAINTING: STREET: (PLACE) The street looked like an unfinished painting. So much of the canvas was still perfectly white, as if waiting for the artists hand to return. The morning light struggled through the murky cloud, but even in its weakness it was enough to blind. The air was of course cold, but Maisy hadn't expected the same dampness that comes before rain. Moving from the overbearing heat of the kitchen to the verandah was like sipping on ice-water in the height of summer, until her lips went blue and she scurried back to the roasting winter vegetables and baking apple pie. (Unknown)

LOOKED LIKE WHITE-HAIRED GIANTS: MOUNTAINS: (PLACE) The towering mountains looked like white-haired giants patrolling the roof of the world (Unknown)

LOOKED LIKE: ARISTOCRAT: (PERSON) She studied the photo. Mason Lord looked like an aristocrat in the photo, with his blade of a nose, dark arched brows, cold blue eyes, and pewter hair, perfectly presented, attending a charity ball. (*RECKONING* by Catherine Coulter)

LOOKED LIKE: BIKER BABE'S MOM: (PERSON) She indeed looked like the biker babe's mom. Her eyes were the same light green color as her kid's. (*POWER PLAY* by Catherine Coulter)

LOOKED LIKE: BOY AFRAID: (PERSON) [He] suddenly looked like a boy, afraid of what had just happened, not wanting to accept it. (*POWER PLAY* by Catherine Coulter)

LOOKED LIKE: BUTTERFLY: (PERSON) With all the media questions, she began to look like a butterfly being stabbed by a dozen pins when they surrounded her. (*QUINN* by Iris Johansen)

LOOKED LIKE: CLASSIC YOUNG PROFESSIONAL: (PERSON) She looked like a classic young professional in a suit and heels, her hair pulled back from her fine-boned face in a chignon. She had vivid green eyes and dark brown hair with lighter highlights added by an expert hand. Her skin was a smooth light cream. (*RECKONING* by Catherine Coulter)

LOOKED LIKE: COLLEGE PROFESSOR: (PERSON) A man in a rumpled blue suit emerged, fumbled for the fare and stepped through the door. He was bespectacled and looked like a college professor, which he once was. America's most popular serious novelist eschewed an offer to carry his bag and walked to the elevator alone. None of the crowd in the lobby noticed him. (*THE WAYWARD BUS* BY John Steinbeck)

LOOKED LIKE: COMPANY VICE PRESIDENT: (PERSON) The door opened and a medium-sized man came in. He looked like Truman and like a vice-president of a company and like a certified public accountant. His glasses were squared off at the corners. His suit was gray and correct, and there was a little gray in his face, too. He was a businessman, dressed like one—looked like one. In his lapel buttonhole there was a lodge pin so tiny that from four feet away you couldn't see what it was at all. His vest was unbuttoned one notch at the bottom. Indeed the bottom button was not intended to be buttoned. A fine gold watch and key chain crossed this vest and ducked in and out of a buttonhole on the way. (*THE WAYWARD BUS* by John Steinbeck)

LOOKED LIKE: CRAP ON PANCAKE: (PERSON) He'd have to be an idiot not to figure something big was going on, and Briscoe didn't look like crap on a pancake. (*VORTEX* by Catherine Coulter)

LOOKED LIKE: CRIME SNDICATE STEREOTYPE: (PERSON) He looked like a mishmash of every Hollywood Eastern European organized crime syndicate stereotype. His hair was perfectly quaffed and held in place with a healthy dose of gel, his beard was full and slightly unkempt, and his dark-blue tracksuit was zipped down far enough at the neck to reveal a heavy hold chain and medallion resting on a full chest of hair. (*OPERATION JOKTAN* by Amir Tsarfati and Steve Yohn)

LOOKED LIKE: DIDN'T COMPROMISE: (PERSON) He sat silently, his hands clasped in front on him on the table. He stared ahead, not happy, shaking his head at the offer of coffee, looking like he didn't compromise often, or wanted to. (*VORTEX* by Catherine Coulter)

LOOKED LIKE: DIPLOMAT: (PERSON) He looked like a diplomat. His smile was so perfect that he must have practiced it in front of a mirror. It was the sort of smile that could mean anything, or more likely, nothing. (*PATRIOT GAMES* by Tom Clancy)

LOOKED LIKE: DRINK: (PERSON) He slugged down a straight whiskey and looked like he was used to this and didn't particularly like it. (*POWER PLAY* by Catherine Coulter)

LOOKED LIKE: DRUNKEN ADMIRAL: (PERSON) I put the hat on the newel post of the banister, and it looked like a drunken admiral if there is such a thing. (*THE WINTER OF OUR DISCONTENT* by John Steinbeck)

LOOKED LIKE: DUDLEY DO-RIGHT OF MOUNTIES: (PERSON) he had undistinguished features, a heavy beard and a lantern jaw that made him look like a dark-haired Dudley Do-Right of the Mounties. (*PATRIOT GAMES* by Tom Clancy)

LOOKED LIKE: EX-HARDLINE MILITARY: (PERSON) The doctor said, "I'll tell you, while I worked on him, I kept hoping he'd pass out, but he looked like ex-hardline military, a Green Beret or a Ranger or something. He was fit and tough, and he dragged his left leg, probably from a war wound. Everything I did seemed quite natural to him, like he'd seen it before. Of course, he didn't want me to give him anything intravenous that could know him out. He had me only use lidocaine, and he took a couple of Vicodin, but he could still function, still hold it together." (*POWER PLAY* by Catherine Coulter)

LOOKED LIKE: FAIRY PRINCESS: WOMAN: The woman was tall, dressed in black pants, a crisp white shirt, black boots on her feet. She looks like a sprite or a redheaded fairy princess with blue eyes, a lovely smile, and no hard edges to her. (*POWER PLAY* by Catherine Coulter)

LOOKED LIKE: FIGHTER: (PERSON) The door opened and a man stepped in. He was a pale, tallow creature, wanting two fingers on the left hand although he did not look much like a fighter. He was not nautical-looking, and yet he had a smack of the sea about him. (*TREASURE ISLAND* by Robert Louis Stevenson)

LOOKED LIKE: FOOD: (PERSON) served on of the tables what looked like decent bar food and a carafe of white wine. (ABANDONED IN DEATH by J. D. Robb)

LOOKED LIKE: FORT AND CASTLE: HOUSE: (PLACE) The house was half gray stone, half log, and looked like a cross between a frontier fort and a small castle. It even had a pair of stone turrets soaring into the blue sky. (*HEARTLAND* by Bethany Campbell)

LOOKED LIKE: FRIAR: (PERSON) ... was bald except for a fringe of silver hair that made him look like a worldly, benevolent friar. (*LOVE UPON THE WIND* by Sally Stewart)

LOOKED LIKE: GIANT HIVE: JERUSALEM: (PLACE) Jerusalem and its great temple were like a giant hive to the Judean bees who appeared in long dusty lines along the inbound roads in the morning and who, after the last evening sacrifices, left in long slow queues, like thousands of dark insects who, after spawning, leave a common time without communicating with each other. (*THE DAY CHRIST WAS BORN* by Jim Bishop)

LOOKED LIKE: HAD BUSINESS TO CONDUCT: (PERSON) The bright sunlight hurt her eyes, made them water, but she tried to look like she had some business as they came out of the alley into the street. (*DESPERATION IN DEATH* by J.D. Robb)

LOOKED LIKE: HAPPY MAN: (PERSON) He smiled at Grissom, who looked like he'd be a happy man if he could get the detective into an alley. (*RECKONING* by Catherine Coulter)

LOOKED LIKE: HAPPY WARRIOR: (PERSON) he looked like he was—a happy warrior. (Unknown)

LOOKED LIKE: HARMLESS OLD DUDE: (PERSON) He was breathing hard as he stepped back. His teeth looked discolored. He looked much older than his fifty-six years. His graying brown hair was thin on his head, a gray stubble dotted his sagging jowls. He looked like a harmless old dude, except for his eyes. Even from twelve feet away, she saw madness in him, bursting to get out. His eyes looked like a deep well of black, and behind those eyes crouched scary things. (*POWER PLAY* by Catherine Coulter)

LOOKED LIKE: HIT BY TRUCK: (PERSON) ... looked like he'd been hit by a truck. (*FINAL TARGET* by Iris Johansen)

LOOKED LIKE: HOLLYWOODE GANGSTER: (PERSON) He wore a bespoke suit, but oddly, he came across looking like a stereotypical Hollywood gangster. (RECKONING by Catherine Coulter)

LOOKED LIKE: KING: (PERSON) The lights dimmed, signaling five minutes until the performance would begin. The audience slowly quieted. The orchestra finished tuning their instruments, sat still in their chairs, ready. The conductor came onstage in his bespoke tux looking like a king, his rooster tail of white hair towering high. He introduced his first violinist and beckoned to Emma. (*RECKONING* by Catherine Coulter)

LOOKED LIKE: MAN: (PERSON) He was a slender young man who did look like Mr. Sullivan. He was a soft-spoken, handsome young man, and he looked scared, really scared. (*POWER PLAY* by Catherine Coulter)

LOOKED LIKE: MATLOCK ON TV: (PERSON) He looked like Matlock in the old TV series, with his silver hair and his comfortable paunch, artfully minimized in a dark pin-striped thousand-dollar Hugo Boss suit, looking pleased with himself, quite happy to be who he was, confident he had closed the case. (*VORTEX* by Catherine Coulter)

LOOKED LIKE: MOST OTHERS: (PERSON) Philip was the merry one. He was short, dark, and to his way of thinking, the long journey through life toward heaven was a most enjoyable experience. He lived in Bethsaida, in Galilee, and there he had a wife and some three daughters and a sister Marianne. He was like, most of the others, simple and credulous, but he was witty and gregarious as well. (THE DAY CHRIST DIED by Jim Bishop)

LOOKED LIKE: MOUSE: (PERSON) Beatrix looked remarkably like a mouse. Her hair was exactly the proper drag shade of brown and ill-kept. Her face was puffy, whether from too much food or too much drink. One couldn't say, because her eyes were hidden behind thick glasses. She dressed in a way that fitted the store exactly—everything she had on was old and out of date. (*PATRIOT GAMES* by Tom Clancy)

LOOKED LIKE: MOVIE SET: BASEMENT: (PLACE) The basement looked like something from a 1940s movie set. There were thick cobwebs everywhere, like Halloween had come early. (*RECKONING* by Catherine Coulter)

LOOKED LIKE: PARTHENON AND MANSION: (PLACE) it looked like a cross between the Parthenon and an antebellum mansion. (*COUNTRY OF THE HEART* by Robyn Donald)

LOOKED LIKE: PHYSICALLY FIT: (PERSON) He was bigger than his father and fit, looked like he tended his body religiously. He had thick dark hair with a dash of white at the temples, a well-maintained mustache. His eyes were opaque, impossible to read, his expression well-controlled. (*RECKONING* by Catherine Coulter)

LOOKED LIKE: PHYSICALLY FIT: (PERSON) This man was potent with women, was so good-looking, even his sour stiff-necked secretary had eyed him like a chocolate bar. He was tall and fit, looked like he could handle himself. His eyes were all cop. (*RECKONING* by Catherine Coulter)

LOOKED LIKE: PIRATE: (PERSON) They saw a big man striding into the unit, wearing a blue shirt and khakis—the Academy uniform—a bomber jacket, and boots. Davis thought the guy looked like a pirate: cocky walk, swarthy, coloring and eyes as dark as his. He knew to his gut there was a brawler lurking beneath that smooth exterior.. (*POWER PLAY* by Catherine Coulter)

LOOKED LIKE: PROPER BOSTON BRAHMIN: (PERSON) He turned to see his uncle standing in the doorway, looking like a proper Boston Brahmin. (*POWER PLAY* by Catherine Coulter)

LOOKED LIKE: QUEEN DOING PENANCE: (PERSON) she carried herself like a queen who agreed to do a period of penance. (*HEARTLAND* by Bethany Campbell)

LOOKED LIKE: QUEEN: WOMAN: (PERSON) ... walked in looking like the queen of the world, exuding arrogance and competence like a potent perfume. (*POWER PLAY* by Catherine Coulter)

LOOKED LIKE: QUEEN: WOMAN: (PERSON) She was a tall, elegant woman in her long black designer gown, similar in age and as beautifully presented as Natalie. Davis thought that she looked and carried herself like the undisputed queen of her kingdom.. (*POWER PLAY* by Catherine Coulter)

LOOKED LIKE: RORSCHACH BLOT :MAN: (PERSON) He was a blank-faced man in his fifties, bald as an egg, a mustard stain on his black tie, like a Rorschach blot. (*THE LAST SECOND* by Catherine Coulter)

LOOKED LIKE: SEEN BEFORE: (PERSON) The doctor said, "I'll tell you, while I worked on him, I kept hoping he'd pass out, but he looked like ex-hardline military, a Green Beret or a Ranger or something. He was fit and tough, and he dragged his left leg, probably from a war wound. Everything I did seemed quite natural to him, like he'd seen it before. Of course, he didn't want me to give him anything intravenous that could know him out. He had me only use lidocaine, and he took a couple of Vicodin, but he could still function, still hold it together." (*POWER PLAY* by Catherine Coulter)

LOOKED LIKE: SERIOUS MAN: (PERSON) he was a slender man in his mid-forties, with eyes so deep set that they almost gave him the look of a raccoon, the kind of eyes that got that way from sixteen-hour days. A sharp dresser, he looked like a very serious man. (*PATRIOT GAMES* by Tom Clancy)

LOOKED LIKE: SLENDER ARISTOCRAT: (PERSON) Her father looked as dapper as ever in a tailored lightweight gray wool suit, a white shirt and darker gray tie, expensive shoes on his long narrow feet. His hair was a beautiful pewter color now, no dye job for him, and with his thin blade of a nose, his lean face etched with high cheekbones, he looked like a slender aristocrat among peasants. (*RECKONING* by Catherine Coulter)

LOOKED LIKE: SOMEONE WITH PRIVATE OXYGEN: (PERSON) he carried an air of danger with him like private oxygen. (*CIRCLE OF FATE* by Charlotte Lamb)

LOOKED LIKE: STRONG: (PERSON) She looked like she could wrestle a crocodile and come out with a crocodile bag over her arm, not a hair out of place. (*RECKONING* by Catherine Coulter)

LOOKED LIKE: THE ABYSS: WOMAN: (PERSON) [she] was wandering aimlessly through the dark alleys. The moonlight illuminated her path, the wind played with her hair. Her pale skin and dry lips and her black hair like the abyss, froze me in place. (REDDIT WRITER'S GROUP posting)

LOOKED LIKE: THIEF: BOY: (PERSON) He didn't look like a thief, the slim, young boy just shy of a growth spurt with a mop of wavy brown hair and heavy-lidded deep blue eyes that could radiate innocence. (*NIGHTWORK* by Nora Roberts)

LOOKED LIKE: THUG: (PERSON) The man followed them into the car, closed the back door, and locked it. His Beretta was aimed at the agent, center mass. She saw he was young, maybe mid-thirties, his features hard, black scruff on his face he must have thought made him look sexy, but didn't. It only made him look more like a thug. (*RECKONING* by Catherine Coulter)

LOOKED LIKE: WANTED TO SHOOT THEM: (PERSON) He sent his daughter a look, then shook his head at her, but said nothing. She stepped back, but looked like if she'd had a gun she'd shoot them on the spot. (*RECKONING* by Catherine Coulter)

LOOKED LIKE: WASHED-OUT LITTLE RAT: (PERSON) Without make-up, she looked like a washed-out little rat. (*THE WAYWARD BUS* by John Steinbeck)

LOOKED LIKE: WISE OWL: (PERSON) Known as a political whiz, he looked like a wise owl in round glasses and neatly trimmed goatee. (*VORTEX* by Catherine Coulter)

LOOKED LIKE: WOMAN WHO FACED LIFE HEAD-ON: (PERSON) Wearing a red suite with matching red fingernails, she seemed like a woman who faced life head-on and loved every minute of it. (*RECKONING* by Catherine Coulter)

LOOKS LIKE: HAND BONES BROKEN: (PERSON) Curley sat down on the floor, looking in wonder at his crushed hand. Slim and Carlson bent over him. Then Slim straightened up and regarded Lennie with horror. "We got to get him in to a doctor," he said. "Looks to me like ever' bone in his han' is bust." (*OF MICE AND MEN* by John Steinbeck)

LOVE: (PERSON) her love poured out on her children and nourished them like rain on dry soil. She was a good mother. (Author)

LOVEMAKING: (PERSON) ... her parents' lovemaking was tasteful and precise; rather like the well-choreographed and traditional ballets they both so enjoyed. (*JEWELS OF THE SUN* by Nora Roberts)

LOW SKY: LIKE CEILING: (THING) In December the sky can lower like a ceiling, as if the lazier snowflakes have arranged the shortest distance to fall. Even when the sky is blue, the blue has a chilling sparkle, like ice, or diamonds on the fingers of a dowager. At night the sky expands, the stars blaze, like jewels on black velvet. The sky on a clear December night is urgent with signals and promises. No matter how cold the earth may get, here is light. Here is heat. Here is the hearth of the universe. Here is the evidence of regeneration. *(Melvin Maddocks, THE CHRISTIAN SCIENE MONITOR)*

LOW SKY: LIKE GRAY CEILING: (THING) the December sky lowered like a gray ceiling giving the snowflakes a short distance to fall (Unknown)

LOWER HEAD: LIKE ANGRY MILK-COW: (PERSON) She lowered her head like an angry milk-cow. (*THE WAYWARD BUS* by John Steinbeck)

LOYAL: MAN: (PERSON) He was like a trained dog, with doglike loyalty, but he lacked imagination. (*PATRIOT GAMES* by Tom Clancy)

LUMBER: ACTION: WATCH: (PERSON) At one point he stopped dead, mouth falling open in shock as he watched a bear—an actual bear—lumber across the road like he was heading home after a hard day's work. (*NIGHTWORK* by Nora Roberts)

LUNCHED: MALE: MAN: (PERSON) He lunched like a king at a banquet. (*Unknown*)

LUPINES LAY DOWN: LIKE GRAIN: (THING) The rain stripped the petals of the golden poppies and the lupines lay down like grain, too fat, too heavy, to hold up their wet heads. (*THE WAYWARD BUS* by John Steinbeck)

LURK: LIKE PIT BOSS IN CASINO: (THING) Lurking like a pit boss in a casino. (*DAN BONGINO SHOW* podcast June 18, 2024)

MAGNIFICENT SUNSET: ALMOST LIKE ONE AT SEA: (THING) The sunset was magnificent, almost like one at sea. The sky was clear of the usual urban pollution, and the distant dunes gave a crisp, if crenelated line for the sun to slide behind. (*PATRIOT GAMES* by Tom Clancy)

MAN LIVED: LIKE MONARCH: (PERSON) The urbane man lived in a sophisticated style like the monarch of a thriving kingdom. (*COUNTRY OF THE HEART* by Robyn Donald)

MARK ROUTE: LIKE ARROWS: PATH: (PLACE) They were like arrows marking the path. (Author)

MEMORY ALBUM: LIKE FOOTNOTE: ROOM: (PLACE) The room was a memory album of other rooms, bits and pieces of other lives like footnotes. *(THE WINTER OF OUR DISCONTENT by John Steinbeck)*

MESSY: LIKE NUKED TOY STORE: HOUSE: (PLACE) The house looked like a Toys 'R Us [store] that got nuked. (*PATRIOT GAMES* by Tom Clancy)

MINIMIZE THREAT: SEEM LIKE FLOCK OF HOOLIGANS: (THING) a billion people with a strong, driving economy, right on the border, hungry for land, and with a racial hatred of all Russians that could make Hitler's fascist legions seem like a flock of football hooligans.. (*THE CARDINAL OF THE KREMLIN* by Tom Clancy)

MIST RISING: LIKE VAPOR FROM MOORS: (THING) ... a beautiful spring morning as a mist rose from the warm ground and trailed across the yard like a vapor from the moors. *(OUT TO CANAAN by Jan Karon)*

MOON SHADOW: LIKE BRUSH STROKE ACROSS CANVAS OF CONTINENT: ECLIPSE: (THING) ...millions of Americans were transfixed by the spectacle of a total solar eclipse midday Monday, as the moon's shadow raced from coast to coast like a brush stroke across the canvas of the continent." (Unknown)

MOON: LIKE SLIVERS OF BROKEN GLASS: (PERSON) She looked at him and nodded. In her pupils, the reflected light of the moon looked like slivers of broken glass . (*POWER PLAYS POLITIKA* by Tom Clancy and Martin Greenberg)

MOONLIGHT: LIKE CURVED NEEDLE: (THING) The moon was only four days grown like a thickened curved surgeon's needle, but it was strong enough to pull the tide into the cave mouth. (*THE WINTER OF OUR DISCONTENT* by John Steinbeck)

MOUNTAINS OUTLINED IN RED: LIKE DRAGON'S TEETH: (THING) The sun would soon rise, earlier there because of the lower latitude, and the jagged spires of mountains were outlined in red, like dragons' teeth. (*THE CARDINAL OF THE KREMLIN* by Tom Clancy)

MOUTH SQUARE: LIKE SOME MOVIE STARS: (PERSON) mouth look square, like some of the movie stars (Unknown)

MOVE: CLEAVE: (PERSON) As the sun eased toward high peaks in the west, she cleaved through the clouds like a boat through the sea, and the wind on her face tasted fresh and crisp. (*ABANDONED IN DEATH* by J. D. Robb)

MOVE: GOVERNMENT: SLOW: (THING) Anything dependent upon the government moves like molasses on a winter day. (Larry Arnn, President Hillsdale College, IMPRIMIS November 2024)

MOVE: LIKE CRIPPLED STORK: AIRCRAFT: (THING) The fighter moved off the runway like a crippled stork. A minute later she was in the air, a silky smooth feeling of pure power enveloping the pilot at the jet's nose was pointed at the sky. (*RED STORM RISING* by Tom Clancy)

MOVE: LIKE LITTLE WAVES: SQIRRELS: (PLACE) In the reedy edges of the inner waters, the mallards nested and brought out their young flotillas, muskrats dug communities and swam lithely in the early morning. The ospreys hung, aimed, and plummeted on fish, and sea gulls carried clams and scallops high in the air and dropped them to break them open for eating. Some otters still clove the water like secret furry whispers; rabbits poached in the gardens and gray squirrels moved like little waves in the streets of the village. Cock pheasants flapped and coughed their crowing. Blue herons poised in the shallow water like leggy rapiers and at night the bitterns cried out like lonesome ghosts. *(THE WINTER OF OUR DISCONTENT by John Steinbeck)*

MOVE: LIKE SHADOWS OF CLOUD: CAT: (THING) "The wild cats crept in Source: the fields at night, but they did not mew at the doorstep any more. They moved like shadows of a cloud across the moon, into the rooms to hunt the mice." *(THE GRAPES OF WRATH by John Steinbeck)*

MOVED SLOWLY: LIKE MEN RELUCTANT TO FINISH JOURNEY: (PERSON) The eleven men came through the pass slowly, like men reluctant to finish a journey. They were robed in white, their sandals powdery from the chalky dust, their faces molded with concern. They were part of the final trickle of humans pouring into the walled city of Jerusalem for the Passover observance. (*THE DAY CHRIST DIED* by Jim Bishop)

MOVEMENT: (PERSON) Snail-like relentlessness, the inevitability of their approach. (*THE GUNS OF NAVORONE* by Alistair Maclean)

MOVING: LIKE SLIPPING ON ICE-WATER: (PLACE) The street looked like an unfinished painting. So much of the canvas was still perfectly white, as if waiting for the artists hand to return. The morning light struggled through the murky cloud, but even in its weakness it was enough to blind. The air was of course cold, but Maisy hadn't expected the same dampness that comes before rain. Moving from the overbearing heat of the kitchen to the verandah was like sipping on ice-water in the height of summer, until her lips went blue and she scurried back to the roasting winter vegetables and baking apple pie. (Unknown)

MUDDY: LIKE TORRENT OF CHOCOLATE: RIVER: (PLACE) The Missouri River was so muddy it looked like a torrent of chocolate. (*HEARTLAND* by Bethany Campbell)

MUFFLED VOICE: LIKE TALKING THROUGH WADDED HANDKERCHIEF: (THING) It was a man with a deep voice, but it sounded muffled, like he was talking through a wadded-up handkerchief. (*POWER PLAY* by Catherine Coulter)

MURMUR SOUND: LIKE WHISPERS AND MURMURS OF CONSPIRATORS: (THING) ...sound...like the whispers and murmurs of conspirators. (Unknown)

MUSIC SOUND: LIKE HEARING STRANGE FOREIGN LANGUAGE: (THING) Listening to an album on an ordinary system was like hearing a strange foreign language—you recognize the noise, but grasp no deeper meaning. *(SUCCESS, November 1987)*

MUSTACHE: LIKE SHADOW OF COMING EVENT: (PERSON) He had a mustache like the shadow of a coming event. (Readers Digest *TOWARD MORE PICTURESQUE SPEECH*)

MUSTACHE: LIKE SMOOSHED CATERPILLAR: (PERSON) His eyebrows beetled together over the beady eyes in his egg-shaped head. The mustache he'd decided to grow looked like a smooshed caterpillar over his tight, turned-down mouth. (*ABANDONED IN DEATH* by J. D. Robb)

MUZZLE TALISMAN: LIKE SUCKLING PUPPY: (THING) She had the magic talisman mound of stone in her hands, caressing it with her fingers, petting it as though it were alive. She pressed it against her unformed breast, placed it on her cheek below her ear, nuzzled it like a suckling puppy, and she hummed a low song like a moan of pleasure and of longing. It was mother, lover, and child, in her hands. (*THE WINTER OF OUR DISCONTENT* by John Steinbeck)

NAÏVE: LIKE DON'T KNOW LIMITS OF OWN KNOWLEDGE: (PERSON) He was like someone who doesn't know the limits of his own knowledge. (*RECKONING* by Catherine Coulter)

NAME FINGS: LIKE BELL: (PERSON) ... in my heart your name rings like a bell. (*THE WINTER OF OUR DISCONTENT* by John Steinbeck)

NEEDLE: (PERSON) He felt it was his job to keep prickling the elites like sticking a pin into an elephant's hide until either his career would end or until they'd be pestered into asking for peace. (*THE CAPTAIN FROM CONNECTICUT* by C.S. Forester)

NERVOUS: (PERSON) He leapt up; a gawky young man who plunged about like a nervous horse, his body never quite under his control. (*CIRCLE OF FATE* by Charlotte Lamb)

NEW: LIKE UNSEEN OR IMAGINED: COUNTRYSIDE: (PLACE) She watched the rolling jade-green fields flow past. Their impossible brilliance was matched and made more intense by the seemingly endless sweep of flawless blue sky. It was country unlike any she had seen or even imagined. (*HEARTLAND* by Bethany Campbell)

NOSE: (PERSON) a large nose like Jimmy Durante (Unknown)

OBSTINATE ACTION: LIKE MONKEY FLINGING POO: (PERSON) is obstinate actions were like a monkey flinging its poo at people on the sidewalk. (*LEAGUE OF POWER* 8Feb2024)

OCEAN GLITTERED: LIKE HAMMERED SILVER: (THING) Dawn came up without any thunder. It was all golden green, dark of heather and pale with fern and yellowy red with wet dune sand, and the ocean glittering like hammered silver. (*THE WINTER OF OUR DISCONTENT* by John Steinbeck)

OCHRE AND WHITE PEAKS: LOOKED ALIKE: WILDERNESS: (PLACE) The wilderness is a barren place in the mountains, where nothing of consequence grows and the tiny peaks look alike, ochre and white and chalky, a place where bandits await the ornate sedan chairs and the sun smites the walker until the sweat causes a man's legs to itch and softening the straps of his sandals. (*THE DAY CHRIST WAS BORN* by Jim Bishop)

OLD AND WOODEN HOMES: LIKE THEY EVER WERE: HOUSE: (PLACE) The homes are like they ever were, old and wooden. "Heritage," I think we used to say. His house stands on a corner, red painted cedar siding and a shingle roof he's going to wish he replaced before the world changed. There is no door at ground level but the wooden steps lead up to a balcony. I know better than to enter the front yard, no-one lives here without some kind of security. (Unknown)

OPEN SUDDENLY: LIKE SLIGHT OF HAND: MOUNTAIN PASS: (PLACE) The entrance to the pass opened suddenly, like a slight of hand, out of nowhere. (Unknown)

OPEN: LIKE DAMMED-UP FLOOD: (PERSON) The guards opened the gates and the people poured in like a dammed-up flood. (*THE DAY CHRIST DIED* by Jim Bishop)

OPENED UP: LIKE ROSES BLOOMING: (PERSON) The girl spoke Italian to the couple and they opened like roses blooming. When Emma spoke her few Italian phrases, the couple beamed at her. (*RECKONING* by Catherine Coulter)

ORPHANED: LIKE LONELY LITTLE TOWN: (PLACE) like a lonely little town orphaned by the freeway. (Unknown)

OUT-OF-CONTROL: LIKE TIDAL WAVE: (THING) Events were spiraling out-of-control, like a tidal wave gathering force and speed. (*POWER PLAY* by Catherine Coulter)

OUTSTRETCH: ACTION: GIVE: (PERSON) George's hand remained outstretched imperiously. Slowly, like a terrier who doesn't want to bring a ball to its master, Lennie approached, drew back, approached again. George snapped his fingers sharply, and at the sound Lennie laid the mouse in his hand. (*OF MICE AND MEN* by John Steinbeck)

OVERPOWER: LIKE SENDING: (PERSON) Sending a large group of soldiers to arrest him was like sending a major general and two brigades to apprehend a cripple. (*MIDNIGHT SHADOWS* by Nora Roberts)

PAIN: LIKE VIOLIN: (PERSON) Each minute required sixty slow steps to cross the faces of the condemned. With each second, the pain mounted. But death was not ready. The arms, the limbs, the torso screamed with pain, the nerves pulled across a bridge like that on a violin, and the nerve ends were screwed tighter and tighter. (*THE DAY CHRIST DIED* by Jim Bishop)

PAMPER: LIKE FAITHFUL HORSE: (THING) The car was pampered like a faithful horse that had jumped all the fences properly. (*PATRIOT GAMES* by Tom Clancy)

PAMPER: LIKE ROYAL CAT: (THING) her mother had two ill-tempered Siamese cats that were pampered like royalty. (*JEWELS OF THE SUN* by Nora Roberts)

PAYDAY: LIKE ACADEMY AWARDS: (THING) Payday at his house was like the Academy Awards. His wife would say, "May I have the envelope please." (*Reader's Digest TOWARD MORE PICTURESQUE SPEECH*)

PEEK THROUGH IVY: LIKE MISCHIEVOUS EYES: HOUSE: (PLACE) it was sitting on the crest of the hill, positioned, staring over the marshes. Its hair was green ivy, swamping it in a green façade, French windows peeking through the green like mischievous eyes through a long fringe. The house looked almost as if it was natural as it was blended into the green garden by the ivy clambering up its side. The skin of red bricks looked as if they had been burnt by the sun. The garden sloping steeply down towards the marsh as if it was a pedestal for the house: presenting it in all its grandness. The house was beautifully symmetrical, two wings stretching to each side reaching out to touch the fences on each side. The house positioned over the marshes with a view of the river drunkenly meandering its way to the edge of the horizon. (Unknown)

PEER: LIKE CAT WAITING: (PERSON) He hung about just inside the doorway, peering round the corner like a cat waiting for a mouse. (by Robert Louis Stevenson)

PEER: LIKE DARK EYES: CAVE: (PLACE) In the cliff of sandstone are erosion caves cut by the wind and dug out by animals.

The caves looked like dark eyes peering out of the yellow cliff. (*THE WAYWARD BUS* by John Steinbeck)

PENETRATE: LIKE IT USUALLY DOES: FOREST: (PLACE) The woods accelerated the twilight, shrinking what would normally take an hour into just a few minutes. When Tessa entered on the rutted path, carefully avoiding the hoof-sized frozen pools, the light had faded so little she didn't even notice the difference. It wasn't a long trek, it was muddier for sure but it would get her home twenty minutes earlier. Her eyes adjusted slowly to the encroaching gloom and it wasn't for ten minutes that she realized the sun wasn't penetrating the leaves like it usually does and everything was a hue darker than it should be. She picked up her pace but in only five more minutes it was undeniably dark, she could no longer avoid the ruts and her ankle twisted painfully when she made a misstep. The trees had become silhouettes, the air was colder and the gaiety of the woodland had been replaced with a sense of isolation. Her heart pounded in a way that had nothing to do with the exertion of walking. Soon the path and her own feet melted into blackness... (Unknown)

PERFECT: ISLAND: (PLACE) Three Sisters Island was still and white and perfect, like one of the snow globes on the shelf at Island Treasures [tourist shop]. (*HEAVEN AND EARTH* by Nora Roberts)

PERSISTENT: LIKE WATCHING PARADE: (PERSON) It was like watching a parade go by, just standing and watching it go by and knowing what the next float would be but watching for it just the same. (*THE WINTER OF OUR DISCONTENT* by John Steinbeck)

PILE UP: LIKE PIES: STORE: (PLACE) "Along 66 the hamburger stands. Board-and-bat shacks. There were two gasoline pumps in front, a screen door, a long bar, stools, and a foot rail. Near the door three slot machines, showing through glass the wealth in nickels three bars will bring. And beside them, the nickel phonograph with records piled up like pies, ready to swing out to the turntable and play dance music. "Ti-pi-ti-pi-tin," "Thanks for the Memory," Bing

Crosby, Benny Goodman. At one end of the counter a covered case; candy cough drops, caffeine sulphate called Sleepless, No-Doze; candy, cigarettes, razor blades, aspirin, Brome-Seltzer, Alka-Seltzer. The walls decorated with posters, bathing girls, blondes with big breasts and slender hips and waxen faces, in white bathing suits, and holding a bottle of Coca-Cola and smiling—see what you get with a Coca-Cola. Long bar, and salts, peppers, mustard pots, and paper napkins. Beer taps behind the counter, and in back the coffee urns, shiny and steaming, with glass gauges showing the coffee level. And [there were] pies in wire cages and oranges in pyramids of four. And little piles of Post Toasties, corn flakes, stacked up in designs. The signs on cards, picked out with shining mica: Pies Like Mother Used to Make. Credit Makes Enemies, Let's Be Friends. Ladies May Smoke But Be Careful Where You Lay Your Butts. Eat Here and Keep Your Wife for a Pet. Down at one end the cooking plates, pots of stew, potatoes, pot roast, roast beef, gray roast pork waiting to be sliced. Minnie or Susy or Mae, middle-aging behind the counter, hair curled and rouge and powder [applied] on a sweating face; taking orders in a soft low voice, calling them out to the cook with a screech like a peacock; mopping the counter with circular strokes, polishing the big shining coffee urns. The cook is Joe or Carl or Al, hot in a white coat and apron, beady sweat on white forehead, below the white cook's cap, moody, rarely speaking, looking up for a moment at each new entry. Wiping the griddle, slapping down the hamburger. He repeats Mae's orders gently, scrapes the griddle, and wipes it down with burlap. Moody and silent."
(THE GRAPES OF WRATH by John Steinbeck)

PLAY POKER: LIKE HIMSELF: (PERSON) He was a businessman, president of a medium-sized corporation, and he was never alone. His business was conducted by groups of men who worked alike, thought alike, and even looked alike. His lunches were with men like himself who joined together in clubs so that no foreign element or idea could enter. His religious life was again his lodge and his church, both of which were screened and protected. One night a week he played poker with men so exactly like himself that the game was fairly even, and from this fact his group was convinced that they were very fine poker players. Wherever he went he was not one man but a unit in a corporation, a unit in a club, in a lodge, in a church, in a political party. His thoughts and ideas were never subjected to criticism since he willingly associated only with people like himself. He read a newspaper written by and for his group. He books that came into his house were chosen by a committee which deleted material that might irritate him. He hated foreign countries and foreigners because it was difficult to find his counterpart in them. He did not want to stand out from his group. He would like to have risen to the top of it and be admired by it, but it would not occur to him to leave it. (*THE WAYWARD BUS* by John Steinbeck)

  PLAY: ACTION: PLAY CARDS: (PERSON) Played cards like a casino dealer. (*Author*)

  PLAY: ACTION: PLAY CARDS: (PERSON) Played cards like a professional. (*Author*)

  PLAY: LIKE DEMON ANGELS: (PERSON) The musicians were shoehorned into the front booth, taking the space over in their workingmen's clothes and boots as they played like demon angels. (*JEWELS OF THE SUN* by Nora Roberts)

  PLAY: LIKE FIDDLE: (PERSON) He played the media like a fiddle again with his comments to … (*RENEWED RIGHT.COM* podcast 2Dec2023)

  PLAY: LIKE GOLF: (PERSON) like playing put-put golf on the world stage. (*LEAGUE OF POWER* 8Feb2024)

  PLAY: LIKE PRO: (PERSON) "He's first rate at cat and mouse, played the game like a pro, hardly any tells, but I saw them." (*VORTEX* by Catherine Coulter)

  PLOD: LIKE LITTLE ARMADILLOS: (THING) The sun lay on the grass and warmed it, and in the shade under the grass the insects moved, ants and ant lions to set traps for them, grasshoppers to jump into the air and flick their yellow wings for a second, sow bugs like little armadillos, plodding restlessly on many tender feet. *(THE GRAPES OF WRATH* by John S*teinbeck)*

PLUNGE INTO SUNLIGHT: LIKE TWO SWIMMERS HASTENING TO GET TO SHORE: (THING) "They hesitated on the edge of the shade and then they plunged into the yellow sunlight like two swimmers hastening to get to shore." *(THE GRAPES OF WRATH* by John Steinbeck*)*

PODCAST: LIKE DANDELION CAUGHT IN WIND: (THING) This (podcast) will be like a dandelion caught in the wind spreading the seeds of the good news of the Gospel throughout the world. (Amir Tsarfati, *BEHOLD ISRAEL*, 2-9 May 2024)

POKE: ACTION: ANGER: (PERSON) like poking a bear. (*Author*)

POLITICS: LIKE CAR: (THING) Politics without compromise is like a car without a gearbox; it can look quite elegant but you won't get anything out of it. (Neil Kinnock)

POLITICS: LIKE FAST FOOD: (THING) The American political system is like fast food— mushy, insipid, made out of disgusting parts of things...and everybody wants some. (P.J. O'Rourke)

POLITICS: LIKE FOOTBALL COACH: (THING) Being in politics is like being a football coach. You have to be smart enough to understand the game, and dumb enough to think it's important. (Eugene McCarthy)

POLITICS: LIKE GAMBLING: (THING) There is no gambling like politics. (Benjamin Disraeli)

POLITICS: LIKE LABRYINTH: (THING) Politics are like a labyrinth, from the inner intricacies of which it is even more difficult to find the way of escape than it was to find the way into them. (William E. Gladstone)

POLITICS: LIKE WAKING UP: (THING) Politics is like waking up in the morning. You never know whose head you will find on the pillow. (Winston Churchill)

POLITICS: LIKE WOLVES: (THING) In politics you must always keep running with the pack. The moment that you falter and they sense that you are injured, the rest will turn on you like wolves. (R. A. Butler)

POPPY PETALS LAY ON GROUND: LIKE GOLD COINS: (THING) The gray wall of water from the cloudburst obscured the hills and there was a dark, metallic light with it. The heads of the lupines bent down, heavy with water. The petals of the poppies were beaten off and lay on the ground like gold coins. The already wet ground could absorb no more water, and little rivulets started immediately for the low places. Meanwhile, the cloudburst roared on the roof of the lunchroom. (*THE WAYWARD BUS* by John Steinbeck)

PORT: LIKE DESERT HEMMED IN BY WATER AND EARTH: (THING) The port was like a detached infected appendix in the abdomen of the coastline. It was like a desert hemmed in by water and earth, but which belonged to neither land nor sea ... a grounded amphibian, a marine metamorphosis, a new formation crafted from dirt, garbage and various odds and ends that the tide carried ashore over the years. (Unknown)

PORT: LIKE DETACHED INFECTED APPENDIX: (THING) The port was like a detached infected appendix in the abdomen of the coastline. It was like a desert hemmed in by water and earth, but which belonged to neither land nor sea ... a grounded amphibian, a marine metamorphosis, a new formation crafted from dirt, garbage and various odds and ends that the tide carried ashore over the years. (Unknown)

POSE: LIKE LEGGY RAPIERS: MARSH: (PLACE) In the reedy edges of the inner waters, the mallards nested and brought out their young flotillas, muskrats dug communities and swam lithely in the early morning. The ospreys hung, aimed, and plummeted on fish, and sea gulls carried clams and scallops high in the air and dropped them to break them open for eating. Some otters still clove the water like secret furry whispers; rabbits poached in the gardens and gray squirrels moved like little waves in the streets of the village. Cock pheasants flapped and coughed their crowing. Blue herons poised in the shallow water like leggy rapiers and at night the bitterns cried out like lonesome ghosts. *(THE WINTER OF OUR DISCONTENT by John Steinbeck)*

POSTURE: LIKE TOTALITARIAN WANNABE: (PERSON) "Politicians who posture like totalitarian wannabes might well be giving us glimpses of their intentions." (Robert W. Malone MD, 29July2023)

POUND: LIKE GOING TO CRACK A RIB: STREET: (PLACE) I have walked these streets my whole life, I know them just the same as if they were etched in my head with a sharp knife, scored in deep like some strange work of art. These are the streets I grew up on and for the most part I'm calm here, at home, on the down low with a steady heartbeat. Not tonight though. Tonight my heart wants out of my chest. It wants to beat free of its cage. It pounds like it's going to crack a rib. My senses are on high alert. Every color is brighter, every noise louder, every stranger a cause to make my heart beat more fiercely still. It's been like that since the bikers came to town, marking out their turf like a wolf pack. I don't even deal drugs but they mean to dominate everyone regardless. They've got Kenny dealing for them already, there goes his grades, and there goes his life. So now the streets that were my salvation spike my adrenaline as good as a shot to the arm. (Unknown)

POUR OUT: LIKE TIDE: (PERSON) It was four o'clock in the afternoon, and government employees were pouring out of buildings like a tide. Cars gridlocked the streets and people were thick on the sidewalks and at the crosswalks, *(POWER PLAY* by Catherine Coulter)

PRETTY: ACTION: (PERSON) He stopped awhile at Lake Norman—it was no Lake Michigan, but pretty enough. He liked the trees, and the December quiet while he ate a burrito he'd picked up at a mini-mart. (*NIGHTWORK* by Nora Roberts)

PREVENT SEEING: LIKE BLINDFOLDING EAGLE: (PERSON) it was like blindfolding an eagle. (*COUNTRY OF THE HEART* by Robyn Donald)

PRICE INCREASE: LIKE GREASED PIG ON ROLLER SKATES: (THING) Price increases like a greased pig on roller skates coming down a solid glass mountain, only slightly faster. (Comment by Robert Sheckley and referenced on *QUORA* 14Sep2023)

PRISON: LIKE BEING IN COCOON: (PERSON) ... had a lot of time to think while in prison. It was like being in a cocoon and turning into a butterfly. (*FINAL TARGET* by Iris Johansen)

PROGRESS: LIKE PERSONALITY: (PERSON) Her progress, like her personality, was swift and embracing. (INSIGHT Article by Jane Addams Allen)

PROTECT: LIKE ARMOR PLATING: (PERSON) her cool front was like armor plating. (*BEYOND HER CONTROL* by Jessica Steele)

PROTRUDE: LIKE CARTOON CHARACTER: (PERSON) He had large ears that stuck out like Disney's cartoon character, Dumbo. (Unknown)

PROTRUDE: LIKE PARABOLIC REFLECTORS: (PERSON) His ears stuck out like parabolic reflectors. (Unknown)

PROTRUDE: LIKE SEASHELLS: (PERSON) His ears were not very large, but they stood out sharply from his head like seashells, or in the position a man would hold them with his hands if he wanted to hear more clearly. (*THE WAYWARD BUS* by John Steinbeck)

PUFFING: LIKE LANDED FISH: (PERSON) After five minutes of running, he was puffing like a landed fish. (*THE CARDINAL OF THE KREMLIN* by Tom Clancy)

PULSE BEAT: LIKE CORNERED THING IN VEIN: (THING) Inside her wrist her pulse beat like a cornered thing in the blue prison of her vein. (*HEARTLAND* by Bethany Campbell)

PUMP: LIKE GIANT PRAYING MANTISES: (THING) Oil pumps rhythmically nodding like giant praying mantises. (*Reader's Digest TOWARD MORE PICTURESQUE SPEECH*)

PURSUE: LIKE DOG: (PERSON) She pursued a story like a dog pursues a rabbit. (*ABANDONED IN DEATH* by J. D. Robb)

PUSH GREEN LEAVES INTO SKY: LIKE GREY AND BROWN CAMOFLAGE: (THING) fast-growing fragile Eucalyptus trunks pushed their green cover into the sky like grey and brown camouflage. (Unknown)

PUSHING WIND: LIKE MORNING YAWN: (THING) March winds pushing at the air like a morning yawn. (Unknown)

QUESTIONS RAPPED: LIKE BULLET FROM GUN: (THING) The question rapped at her like a bullet from a gun. (*LOVE UPON THE WIND* by Sally Stewart)

QUIET MAN: LIKE HIS DAD: (PERSON) There was another cousin to Jesus in the group at the Passover supper, and this was Jude. He was not a prominent figure among the apostles, and little is known of him. He was, it is believed by many, the brother of James of Alphaeus, although others contend that he was the son of James. He was called Jude, Jude-Thaddaeus, and Judas of James—meaning Judas, the son of James. Like James, Jude was a quiet man, almost introspective, and yet, in the years ahead, Jude would preach the testament of Jesus with a violent passion in Arabia, Mesopotamia, Persia and Syria where, in time, he would be murdered. (*THE DAY CHRIST DIED* by Jim Bishop)

RAIN STREAMING ON DECK: LIKE CATARACT IN SCUPPERS: (THING) There was a warning flap from the sails of his boat and then the squall was close upon them. Heavy fluky gusts of wind and torrential warm rain swept over the boat, heavy as if from a shower-bath, drumming on the deck and streaming like a cataract in the scuppers. (*THE CAPTAIN FROM CONNECTICUT* by C.S. Forester)

RAIN WHISKS: LIKE HEAVY BROOM: (THING) A sheet of rain whisked over the roof like a heavy broom and left silence as it moved on, and almost immediately another flat of rain took its place. (*THE WAYWARD BUS* by John Steinbeck)

RAP WITH STICK: LIKE HANDSPIKE: (PERSON) The seaman came plodding to the inn door, his sea-chest following behind him in a handbarrow; a tall, strong, heavy, nut-brown man; his tarry pigtail falling over the shoulders of his soiled blue coat; his hands ragged and scarred, with black, broken nails; and the saber cut across one cheek, a dirty, livid white. I remember him looking round the cover and whistling to himself as he did so, and then breaking out in that old sea-song that he sand so often afterward: "Fifteen men on the dead man's chest.... Yo-ho-ho, and a bottle of rum!" in the high, old tottering voice that seemed to have been tuned and broken at the captain bars. Then he rapped on the door with a bit of stick like a handspike that he carried. (*TREASURE ISLAND* by Robert Louis Stevenson)

REACHING: LIKE FINGERS: (PERSON) He stood in front of her, his dark eyes reaching deep into her like fingers, wrapping around her very being. (*POWER PLAY* by Catherine Coulter)

RECLINE: LIKE ANACONDA SNAKE: (PERSON) He ate so much he wanted to lie around for two hours like a Brazilian anaconda. (*THE RADIO BOYS AT MOUNTAIN PASS* by Allen Chapman)

RED SUNLIGHT: LIKE DUSK: (THING) The dawn came, but no day. In the gray sky a red sun appeared, a dim red circle that gave a little light, like dusk; and as that day advanced, the dusk slipped back toward darkness, and the wind cried and whimpered over the fallen corn. (*THE GRAPES OF WRATH* by John Steinbeck)

REFLECT SOUND: LIKE ANGLED PANE OF GLASS: (THING) Water was a fine medium for carrying sound energy, far more efficient at it than air, but it had its own rules. One hundred feet below the submarine was "the layer," a fairly abrupt change in water temperature. Like an angled pane of glass, it allowed some sound to pass through, but reflected most of it. Some of the energy would be ducted between layers, retaining its intensity for an enormous distance. (*RED STORM RISING* by Tom Clancy)

REFLECT: LIKE BILLARD BALL BOUNCNG OFF RAIL: (THING) The solar flare's high-energy particles reflected off the submarine hulls, like a billiard ball bouncing off a rail. They scattered in all directions, and unlike visible light waves, water didn't reabsorb them. Satellites circling the earth captured a portion of those bounced reflections, and she was able to plot the sparkles, creating a map showing every submarine in the oceans. (*UNDETECTED* by Dee Henderson)

RELEASE: LIKE LETTING GO: (PERSON) letting him off the hook was like letting go of a heavy weight. (*CIRCLE OF FATE* by Charlotte Lamb)

RELEASE: LIKE SCHOOL BOY: (PERSON) He was like a boy released from school. (*TARZAN AT THE EARTH'S CORE* by Edgar Rice Burroughs)

REMEMBER: LIKE DREAM: TOWN: (PLACE) This place seems so foreign now. The narrow streets flow like rivers, winding around hills and fields rather than cutting a Romanesque line through them. For the most part the lanes are one car wide and the corners blind, obscured behind the hawthorn hedgerow that has been growing unchecked through June and July, giddy with the sunshine and rain. I remember the white blooms and how they are so often over hung by spreading trees, darkening in the sunshine faster than I can tan. I recall the bird song and the gentleness of the sun, even in summer. Even the aroma takes me back to my misspent youth. But I've been gone too long and now this is like a half-forgotten dream. The good parts aren't as good as the memory and the bad parts are more frustrating. I'm just not used to it. As much as I want to savor the here and now I can't wait to board the plane for home; back to straight roads and summer heat that cooks your head. (Unknown)

RESENT: ACTION: (PERSON) They didn't speak any more about it, or about anything as they circled the block, and the resentment inside him built like storm clouds. (*NIGHTWORK* by Nora Roberts)

RESPOND: LIKE JUMPING HORSE AT FENCE: The blue-water fishing boat was just over 200 feet long, and she responded to every wave like a jumping horse to a fence. (*RED STORM RISING* by Tom Clancy)

REVEAL: LIKE NOTHING ELSE: TRAIL: (PLACE) These walking trails scale majestic peaks and cross ancient waterways. They traverse vast deserts, lush forests, and snowy evergreens. Spanning more than 55,000 miles, our national trails cover America—and reveal it like nothing else. Oct 2 marks the 50th anniversary of the creation of the National Trails System. Today is encompasses 11 National Scenic Trails, 19 National Historic Trails, and nearly 1,300 National Recreation Trails. *(SOUTHWEST MAGAZINE*, Oct 2018*)*

REVENGE COMING: LIKE FREIGHT TRAIN: (THING) Trump says he's coming for Biden like a freight train. (Unknown)

RIDE UPPER LIP: LIKE CATERPILLAR: (PERSON) A small, carefully trimmed mustache rode his upper lip like a caterpillar, and when he talked it seemed to hump its back. (*THE WAYWARD BUS* by John Steinbeck)

RIPPLE: LIKE OIL: (PERSON) He rode at a steady gallop, the muscular, sweat-slick sides of his steed rippling like oil beneath his stirrup. (*POWER PLAYS POLITIKA* by Tom Clancy and Martin Greenberg)

RISE: BEACH: (PLACE) In dreams, she stood on the beach, where the waves rose like terror. They pounded, black and bitter, on the shore, a thousand mad heartbeats, under a blind sky. (*HEAVEN AND EARTH* by Nora Roberts)

RIVER GLEAMED: LIKE DARK STEEL: (THING) Below the valley was gloomy with gray clouds and rain, and the great loop of the river gleamed like dark steel under the glowering light. (*THE DAY CHRIST WAS BORN* by Jim Bishop)

ROARING SOUND: LIKE KETTLEDRUMS AND SHOTGUN BLASTS: (THING) The powerful shaking and roaring got louder, you could feel it in your bones, a sound like kettledrums and shotgun blasts all mixed up with the greatest wind you ever heard, though there was no wind. But there was the other sound, too, the queer whistling, warbling, fluty sort of sound under the thunder, getting louder by the second. (Unknown)

ROLL AROUND: LIKE PEACH PIT: (PERSON) She wished she didn't sometimes feel that fear rolling around like a peach pit in her belly. (*RECKONING* by Catherine Coulter)

ROLL UP: LIKE OVERFLOWING BATH TUB: BEACH: (PLACE) Under the mist that swirls thicker than hairspray in a beauty pageant prep-room lies sand that shifts under the pressure of my boot. I can't see it, only feel. Out there, only meters away, is the ocean, alive with constant motion and millions of sea-dwellers. Beyond this wall of white I can smell and hear it. The waves are neither the gentle kind that roll up the beach like an overflowing bath tub, nor the crashing kind that turn murky with golden swirling crystals. They move with force but die within a few feet. From them comes the salty smell, that fragrance that conjures fishing fleets and nets of sun-bleached blue cord hanging out to dry. This place could be anywhere, I guess at a stretch this could be some kind of artificial simulation, but it isn't. This is my hometown beach and that is the sea I swam in as a small child. The wind here carries my mother's voice and her sweet kisses. I stand still, face to the breeze and soak it all in. No technology, no gimmicks, just nature. (Unknown)

ROLL: LIKE BOTTLE IN WATER: (THING) The Hispaniola was rolling scuppers under in the ocean swell. The booms were tearing at the blocks, the rudder was banging to and fro, and the whole ship creaking, groaning, and jumping like a manufactory. The ship was being rolled about like a bottle. (*TREASURE ISLAND* by Robert Louis Stevenson)

ROLL: LIKE DICE: (THING) We climbed on stools at the counter and she slid coffee to us without spilling any out into the saucers. A tiny bottle of cream leaned against one cup and she rolled two paper-wrapped cubes of sugar [toward them] like dice. He cried out, "Snake eyes." *(THE WINTER OF OUR DISCONTENT* by John Steinbeck*)*

ROLL: LIKE STATIONARY GROUND SWELLS: LAND: (PLACE) "The land rolled like great stationary ground swells." *(THE GRAPES OF WRATH by John Steinbeck)*

ROLLING WAVES: LIKE OVERFLOWING BATH TUB: (THING) Under the mist that swirls thicker than hairspray in a beauty pageant prep-room lies sand that shifts under the pressure of my boot. I can't see it, only feel. Out there, only meters away, is the ocean, alive with constant motion and millions of sea-dwellers. Beyond this wall of white I can smell and hear it. The waves are neither the gentle kind that roll up the beach like an overflowing bath tub, nor the crashing kind that turn murky with golden swirling crystals. They move with force but die within a few feet. From them comes the salty smell, that fragrance that conjures fishing fleets and nets of sun-bleached blue cord hanging out to dry. This place could be anywhere, I guess at a stretch this could be some kind of artificial simulation, but it isn't. This is my hometown beach and that is the sea I swam in as a small child. The wind here carries my mother's voice and her sweet kisses. I stand still, face to the breeze and soak it all in. No technology, no gimmicks, just nature... (Unknown)

ROOM SMELL: LIKE STALE CIGARETTE SMOKE AND FRIED CHICKEN: (THING) He walked back to his end motel room, unlocked the door, and closed it quietly behind him. The room smelled like stale cigarette smoke and fried chicken.. (*POWER PLAY* by Catherine Coulter)

ROOMS: LIKE WIND TUNNELS: (THING) There was no central heat in the house. In winter the rooms were like wind tunnels and the air smelled damp. (*CIRCLE OF FATE* by Charlotte Lamb)

ROUGH: HAND: (PERSON) He stole a glance at her ... hand. What a strong, shapely hand, neither too large, nor too small, nor red and rough like that of most ranchers' daughters. (*SUNSET PASS* by Zane Grey)

ROUGH: LIKE ROCKY OUTCROP: (PLACE) The ledge was more like a rocky outcrop, rustic and rough. It was in keeping with the building, only three years old but made to look as if it were ancient. The rocks had been trucked in from some quarry up north and the builders had to consult with old-fashioned brick layers to get the rock facade right. It was all steel and concrete underneath of course, but from out here it looked like it just grew right out of the ground. On the ledge should have been pigeons, peering down in the way they do, looking for pedestrians dropping fragments of their breakfasts. But in the frosted dawn-light the ledge is layered with roses, red, white and pink. It could be a romantic gesture from some eccentric billionaire, but it isn't. It's one rose for day of the empresses' life... (Unknown)

ROUGH: LIKE RUBBING SANDPAPER: (PERSON) She wiped his cheek and noticed that he hadn't shaved, and it was like rubbing sandpaper. (*PATRIOT GAMES* by Tom Clancy)

ROUGH: LIKE SLIDING ACROSS STUCCOED TUB: (THING) The ride out will be rough like sliding across a stuccoed tub. (Airline pilot describing turbulence around Denver. May 8, 2024)

RUMBLE SOUND: LIKE CRASH OF NIAGARA FALLS: (THING) Rumble was now like the crash of Niagara Falls combined with the base-throb pounding of a thousand ... the ... electronic whistle made him feel as if the top of his head was going to be sliced off by a band saw. (Unknown)

RUN ACROSS RANGE: LIKE ANIMAL SPINE: MOUNTAIN: (PLACE) A strong mountain range ran across the land from north to south like the spine of some vast animal. *(THE LIVING REED by Pearl S. Buck)*

RUN: LIKE ANTS: He could see the graceful lines of the warship as she was turning hard on the choppy seas, her men running along the deck like ants. *(Tom Clancy, THE HUNT FOR RED OCTOBER)*

RUN: LIKE GREYHOUND: (PERSON) Running is part of who they are, and you can practically feel their sheer joy, when they can take off, like a greyhound out of the chute. (*POWER PLAY* by Catherine Coulter)

RUN: LIKE SCALDED CAT: (PERSON) She raced off like a scalded cat. (Author)

RUN: LIKE SOMEONE WITH PANTS ON FIRE: (PERSON) ... ran like someone with their pants on fire. (Author)

RUSH: FEMALE: WITCH: (PERSON) Slender, with her cloak streaming back like bird-wings, she stood alone on the wind-whipped beach. Alone but for her rage and her grief; and her power; it was that power that filled her now, rushed inside her in wild pounding stroked like a lover gone mad. (*HEAVEN AND EARTH* by Nora Roberts)

SALLIED: ACTION: WALK: (PERSON) ... sallied forth into the sunlight like a man possessed. (*SUNSET PASS* by Zane Grey)

SCAR: LOOKED LIKE PLASTIC: (PERSON) He stretched his right arm, and as usual the scar tissue was stiff, looking like plastic. (*THE CARDINAL OF THE KREMLIN* by Tom Clancy)

SCATTER: LIKE SHEEP: (THING) The convoy of ships scattered like sheep as the enemy approached. (*THE CAPTAIN FROM CONNECTICUT* by C.S. Forester)

SCATTERED WRECKED VEHICLES: LIKE TRASH THROWN FROM CAR WINDOW: (THING) ... proud vehicles manufactured at the greatest expense and skill were scattered on the landscape like trash thrown from a car window. (*RED STORM RISING* by Tom Clancy)

SCATTERED: LIKE SHEEP: (PERSON) John insisted that he should perform the final loving-kindness for his Messiah; Mary could be left with the women. He was ashamed that the other apostles were not present. As the master had warned, they had scattered like sheep when the shepherd was attacked. It grieved John to think that his beloved Jesus might still be in the hands of strangers in these final hours. He said that he would be of service to them; insisted on it. Who better to lay loving hands on the body than the one to whom he had entrusted his Mother? (*THE DAY CHRIST DIED* by Jim Bishop)

SCAVENGED: LIKE VEHICLES: HOUSE: (PLACE) Houses, most in good repair now, and most occupied. Those that couldn't be salvaged had been—like the vehicles—scavenged for parts. Wood, pipes, tiles, wiring ... anything that could be used. On the reclaimed land, beef cattle, milk cows, goats, sheep, a few llamas, more horses grazed behind carefully tended fences. (*THE RISE OF MAGICKS* by Nora Roberts)

SCOWL: LIKE POOL AMATEUR: (PERSON) A scowl creased his angular face. He had scratched like a rank pool amateur. (*POWER PLAYS POLITIKA* by Tom Clancy and Martin Greenberg)

SCREAM: LIKE WOLVES: (PERSON) I remember a story told me long ago. Early in the last century some of my people believed the end of the world was coming at a certain time. They gave away everything, everything they owned but the bed sheets. Those they put on and at the predicted time they went to the hills to meet the End of the World. Dressed in sheets, hundreds of people prayed and sang. The night came and they sang louder and danced and as it got near time there was a shooting star, and everybody screamed. The aunt relaying the story said she could still remember the screaming. Like wolves, like hyenas, although she had never heard a hyena. Then the moment came. White-dressed men and women and children held their breaths. The moment went on and on. The children got blue in the face—and then it passed. It was done and they were cheated out of their destruction. In the dawn they crept down the hill and tried to get back the clothes they had given away, and the pots and pans and their ox and their ass. And she remembered knowing how bad they must have felt. (*THE WINTER OF OUR DISCONTENT* by John Steinbeck)

SCREECHING SOUND: LIKE TRAFFIC ACCIDENT: (THING) ... sign tore loose and went skidding and screeching along sounding like a traffic accident. (*THE WINTER OF OUR DISCONTENT* by John Steinbeck)

SEA WALL: LOOKED LIKE IT HELD BACK SEA: OCEAN: (THING) The sea wall was single-minded blue and looked like it held back a sea that could easily consume the land. It prevented, but didn't tame it. Farther out, ships and freighters on their way to or from port passed sleek sailing boats with their canvas taut. (*AFFAIRE ROYALE* by Nora Roberts)

SECRET: LIKE FAMILY RECIPES THEORY: (THING) Some fishing theories are secret, like family recipes and are respected and respectable. (*THE WINTER OF OUR DISCONTENT* by John Steinbeck)

SECURE: LIKE FORTRESS: HOUSE: (PLACE) The house is one of those ones rich people buy when they get paranoid about having too much money. It's like a fortress, tall gates with more security gadgets than a military compound. Perhaps behind those yellow bricks they feel safe from harm, but I can't help think they've only built themselves a beautiful prison. Either way though, it's none of my concern, I'm just here for the political endorsement Mr. Holden wants. So with a quick check of my hired suit I lean into the intercom and state my business. In moments a security guard is striding over the pea shingle, each footfall marked with a crunch. His weapon is holstered but his face is still serious. This is where he takes my identification and runs background checks. (Unknown)

SECURITY POSTED: LIKE FALCONS WATCHING FOR RABBITS: (THING) Security was incredibly tight. Outside, numerous uniformed police constables stood about in plain sight, small zippered pistol cases dangling from their hands. Others, uniformed and not, stood on the buildings across the street like falcons on the watch for rabbits, except rabbits don't carry machine guns and RPG-7 bazookas. (*PATRIOT GAMES* by Tom Clancy)

SEE WORLD: LIKE HE DID: ROAD: (PLACE) Carl smiled softly. Though the newspapers blew about the street he paid them no mind, they were no more bother than fall leaves, just ugly. He passed the graffiti and the scarred lampposts, barely noticing the beat up old cars. This avenue might be falling apart just as much as it ever was, but he'd found his love and not a thing or a person could ever take that away. The people that passed him didn't irritate him any longer, perhaps one day they would see the world though love's eyes like he did and he hoped so. Ahead was the intersection and his bus stop, he was early. There would be time enough to enjoy the early summer warmth before boarding. The air was sweet and there was no hurry, his world had been cast anew and he was savoring every moment. (Unknown)

SEE: LIKE TRYING TO LOOK THROUGH MURKY WATER: (THING) Seeing the concept was like trying to look through dark, murky water. (Unknown)

SEEM NATURAL: LIKE SEEN BEFORE: (PERSON) The doctor said, "I'll tell you, while I worked on him, I kept hoping he'd pass out, but he looked like ex-hardline military, a Green Beret or a Ranger or something. He was fit and tough, and he dragged his left leg, probably from a war wound. Everything I did seemed quite natural to him, like he'd seen it before. Of course, he didn't want me to give him anything intravenous that could know him out. He had me only use lidocaine, and he took a couple of Vicodin, but he could still function, still hold it together." (*POWER PLAY* by Catherine Coulter)

SEIZE: LIKE SHARK: (PERSON) He threw in the comment about ... and the media seized on it like sharks to chum. (*RENEWED RIGHT.COM* podcast 2Dec2023)

SEND: LIKE INNOCENT DOVES: (PERSON) He said, "I am sending you like sheep among a pack of wolves. Be prudent, then, like serpents; yet for all that, as innocent as doves. Beware of your fellow men; they will try to hand you over to courts of justice and to flog you in their synagogues; you will even be brought before governors and kings for my sake." (*THE DAY CHRIST DIED* by Jim Bishop)

SEND: LIKE SERPENTS: (PERSON) He said, "I am sending you like sheep among a pack of wolves. Be prudent, then, like serpents; yet for all that, as innocent as doves. Beware of your fellow men; they will try to hand you over to courts of justice and to flog you in their synagogues; you will even be brought before governors and kings for my sake." (*THE DAY CHRIST DIED* by Jim Bishop)

SEND: LIKE WOLVES: (PERSON) He said, "I am sending you like sheep among a pack of wolves. Be prudent, then, like serpents; yet for all that, as innocent as doves. Beware of your fellow men; they will try to hand you over to courts of justice and to flog you in their synagogues; you will even be brought before governors and kings for my sake." (*THE DAY CHRIST DIED* by Jim Bishop)

SET OFF WORDS: LIKE FIRECRACKERS: (THING) What is a talisman? Look it up. I did and then I had to look up "occult," "planetary," "celestial," and "amulet." It was always that way. One word set off others like a string of firecrackers. *(THE WINTER OF OUR DISCONTENT* by John Steinbeck)

SHAKE HANDS: LIKE BOSS: (PERSON) A much younger man stood behind him, obviously his subordinate in billable hours, judging by where he stood. He looked dramatic, no other way to put it, with his dark liquid eyes and glossy black hair a bit on the long side. He wore a black turtleneck beneath a black blazer. He was a sharp package, the perfect distraction for a living and breathing jury. He continued to smile when he introduced himself. Like his boss, he did not offer to shake hands. (*POWER PLAY* by Catherine Coulter)

SHAKE: LIKE BABY'S RATTLE: (PERSON) After the incident, he stood shaking like a baby's rattle. (*PATRIOT GAMES* by Tom Clancy)

SHAKE: LIKE DOG: GRAB: (PERSON) Davis grabbed the man's collar and pulled him straight out of the chair and shook him like a dog. (*POWER PLAY* by Catherine Coulter)

SHAPE: LIKE ABSTRACT PAINTING: COUNTRYSIDE: (PLACE) The hills became increasingly frequent; they were verdant and strangely shaped, like something out of a slightly abstract painting. (HEARTLAND by Bethany Campbell)

SHARP AND COLD: ACTION: RUN: (PERSON) Her pace was a fast and disciplined jog, and her breath rushed out in white plumes, and rushed in, sharp and cold as shards of ice. (*HEAVEN AND EARTH* by Nora Roberts)

SHARP SLOPE: LIKE A CUP: FOREST: (PLACE) We turned aside, and climbed the hill through the woods. Velvety green sprigs of dog-mercury were scattered on the red soil. We came to the top of a slope, where the wood thinned...There was a deep little dell, sharp sloping like a cup, and a white sprinkling of flowers all the way down, with white flowers showing pale among the first inpouring of shadow at the bottom. (Unknown)

SHIMMER: LIKE MIRAGE: (PERSON) feeling of belonging seemed to shimmer ahead like a mirage in a desert. (*CIRCLE OF FATE* by Charlotte Lamb)

SHINE: LIKE A MIRROR: ROAD: (PLACE) "Cars pulled up beside the road, engine heads off, tires mended. Cars limping along 66 like wounded things, panting and struggling. Too hot, loose connections, loose bearings, rattling bodies. People in flight along 66. And the concrete road shone like a mirror under the sun, and in the distance the heat made it seem that there were pools of water in the road." *(THE WINTER OF OUR DISCONTENT by John Steinbeck)*

SHINE: LIKE NEW COIN: (PERSON) ... shined like a newly-minted coin. (Author)

SHINED: LIKE BEACON: (PERSON) Natalie's charm and intelligence shined like a beacon compared to her brother's occasional flicker. (*POWER PLAY* by Catherine Coulter)

SHIRT: LOOKED LIKE A SAIL : (PERSON) The old man had strange shoulders, still powerful although very old, and the neck was still strong too and the creases did not show so much when the old man was asleep and his head fallen forward. His shirt had been patched so many times that it looked like the sail and the patches were faded to many different shades by the sun. The old man's head was very old though and with his eyes closed there was no life in his face. The newspaper lay across his knees and the weight of his arm held it there in the evening breeze. He was barefooted. (*THE OLD MAN AND THE SEA* by Ernest Hemingway)

SHIVER: LIKE MAN WITH AGUE: (THING) Only the snow was real with that bone-deep, sub-zero cold that shrouded him from head to toe in a blanket of ice and continuously shook his entire body in violent, uncontrollable spasms of shivering, like a man suffering from ague. (*THE SECRET WAYS* by Alstair MacLean)

SHOOK: LIKE WET DOG: (PERSON) ... shook like a wet dog. (Author)

SHOOT: ACTION: SACRIFICE: (PERSON) And calling for vengeance, shooting it like a bright and deadly arrow from a bow, she who was known as Earth sacrificed her soul. (*HEAVEN AND EARTH* by Nora Roberts)

SHOT OUT: ACTION: LAUGH: (PERSON) Her laughter shot out like bolts, cracked the black bowl of the sky. A torrent of dark rain fell and hissed on the sand like acid. (*HEAVEN AND EARTH* by Nora Roberts)

SHOUT: LIKE IRATE NEIGHBOR: (PERSON) He appeared like an irate neighbor shouting over the fence. (*DAILY NEWS ELECTION SPECIAL* podcast June 16, 2024)

SHUDDER: LIKE REFLECTION: (PERSON) My stone-built earth shuddered like a reflection in water. My long-planned perfect structure turned to dust before my eyes the way a long-buried artifact does when air strikes it. (*THE WINTER OF OUR DISCONTENT* by John Steinbeck)

SHUFFLE: LIKE OLD MAN: (PERSON) ... shuffled along like an old man. (Author)

SIFT: LIKE WHEAT: (PERSON) Satan demanded the surrender of them in order to sift them like wheat. (*THE DAY CHRIST DIED* by Jim Bishop)

SIGH: LIKE TEENAGER: (PERSON) He flicked a smile that made her want to sigh like a teenager. (*MIDNIGHT SHADOWS* by Nora Roberts)

SIGHING BREEZE: LIKE FAIRIES WHISPERING: (THING) The breeze sighed through the tall grass like faeries whispering. (*JEWELS OF THE SUN* by Nora Roberts)

SILENT: LIKE WAITING PREDATORS: CONSTRUCTION EQUIPMENT: (THING) The yellow-painted bulldozer and the big crane that swung the wrecking ball were silent like waiting predators in the early morning. (*THE WINTER OF OUR DISCONTENT* by John Steinbeck)

SING: LIKE CAGED CANARY: (PERSON) ... sang like a canary in a cage. (Author)

SING: LIKE CONFESSING CONVICT: (PERSON) ... sang like a confessing convict. (Author)

SING: LIKE HAPPY BIRD: (PERSON) ... sang like a happy bird greeting a bright morning. (Author)

SINK: ACTION: THINK: (PERSON) the thought made his heart sink like cold lead. (*SUNSET PASS* by Zane Grey)

SIT: LIKE UNDER THUNDERSTORM: (PERSON) sitting next to him was like sitting under the very core of a thunderstorm before it breaks—there was no lightning flash, no crash of thunder, but darkness and threat concentrated for the close at hand. (*CIRCLE OF FATE* by Charlotte Lamb)

SKIN: LIKE ROSE PETALS: (PERSON) skin like white rose petals. (*DESPERATION IN DEATH* by J.D. Robb)

SKIP: LIKE A GIRL: ROAD: (PLACE) It was summer in the city. The avenue was lined with the deep green foliage that stood still in the August heat wave. Lisa dawdled in their shadows before letting the sunrays heat her unguarded shoulders. She loved the heat but the shade in-between gave her the rest-time she needed. As she descended the gentle slope she wanted to skip like she did as a girl, but instead she walked. Twenty somethings just don't skip – right? On every doorstep was a free paper, lying still, in no danger of being blown away. Then from around the corner came the familiar sight of Jack, his head bobbing along, buds popped into his ears. A slow grin spread over her face, a chance to have a little fun. In the otherwise empty street she crossed to the center line, walking a wide arc until she was behind him. Little by little she snuck closer until she could shout "Boo!" He turned with a face that was just priceless before laughing in the way only he could. (Unknown)

SKIP: LIKE STONES OFF WATER: (PERSON) His small, flat eyes, skipped between the two men facing him like stones off the surface of a pond. (*POWER PLAYS POLITIKA* by Tom Clancy and Martin Greenberg)

SKY SPARKLED: LIKE CHILLED ICE: (THING) the blue December sky sparkled like chilled ice (Unknown)

SLEEP: LIKE LAMB: (PERSON) sleeping like lambs. (*LOVE UPON THE WIND* by Sally Stewart)

SLEEP: LIKE LOG: (PERSON) After a great deal of tossing, he slept like a log of wood. (*TREASURE ISLAND* by Robert Louis Stevenson)

SLEEP: LIKE TREE: (PERSON) He was in magnificent health and spirits, eating like a bull, sleeping like a tree, yet he would not enjoy a moment until he heard his old tarpaulin, tramping round the capstans. (*TREASURE ISLAND* by Robert Louis Stevenson)

SLEEPING: LIKE SINKING INTO SNOW DRIFT: (THING) the bed mattress was stuffed with feathers, and sleeping on it was like sinking into a snow drift. (*CIRCLE OF FATE* by Charlotte Lamb)

SLIDE AWAY: ACTION: SICK: (PERSON) He'd known, hadn't he? Inside he'd known. The circles under her eyes were deeper, her energy sliding away like the flesh on her bones. (*NIGHTWORK* by Nora Roberts)

SLOPING: LIKE PYLONS: HARBOR: (PLACE) The sun was below the western hills but a great powdery cloud scooped its light and threw it on the harbor and the breakwater and the sea beyond so that the whitecaps were pink as roses. The piles in the water by the city pier are triple logs, iron-banded at the top and sloping like pylons to shear the winter ice. On top of each one a gull stood motionless; usually a male with white immaculate vest and clean gray wings. I wonder if each one owns his place and can sell or rent it at will. (*THE WINTER OF OUR DISCONTENT* by John Steinbeck)

SLOWLY: LIKE TERRIER RELUCTANT TO GIVE BACK: (PERSON) George's hand remained outstretched imperiously. Slowly, like a terrier who doesn't want to bring a ball to its master, Lennie approached, drew back, approached again. George snapped his fingers sharply, and at the sound Lennie laid the mouse in his hand. (*OF MICE AND MEN* by John Steinbeck)

SMALL: LIKE DOLL HOUSE: HOUSE: (PLACE) saw a narrow dirt-path leading to a tiny red-brick cottage. The cottage was so small it looked more like a doll's house than a human dwelling. The bricks it was built of were old and crumbly and very pale red. It had a grey slate roof and one small chimney, and there were two little windows at the front. Each window was no larger than a sheet of tabloid newspaper and there was clearly no upstairs to the place. On either side of the path there was a wilderness of nettles and blackberry thorns and long brown grass. An enormous oak tree stood overshadowing the cottage. Its massive spreading branches seemed to be enfolding and embracing the tiny building, and perhaps hiding it as well from the rest of the world. (Unknown)

SMELL OF MAN: LIKE OATMEAL AND STRAWBERRIES: (THING) he smelled like oatmeal and strawberries. (*POWER PLAY* by Catherine Coulter)

SMELL: LIKE CHICKEN AND DUMPLINGS: (THING) ... office smelled like chicken and dumplings soaked in strong black coffee—with a dash of cherry from endless fizzes. *(DEVOTED IN DEATH* by J.D. Robb*)*

SMELL: LIKE CRUSTING OF WHITE FROST: (THING) The chilly air smelled like a crusting of white frost. *(THE WINTER OF OUR DISCONTENT* by John Steinbeck)

SMELL: LIKE DIRTY LAUNDRY: (THING) ... smelled like dirty laundry. (Unknown)

SMELL: LIKE FRESH CUT CLOVER: (THING) like new cut clover in the hay field. (Unknown)

SMELL: LIKE FRESH CUT GRASS: (THING) like freshly cut grass. (Unknown)

SMELL: LIKE PICKLE BARREL: (THING) ... smelled like a pickle barrel (Unknown)

SMELL: LIKE POLECAT: (PERSON) She said, "I can smell like a polecat if I want." (*HEARTLAND* by Bethany Campbell)

SMELL: LIKE RAIN: (THING) It smelled like rain. (Author)

SMELL: LIKE RANCID BUTTER: (THING) It's autumn in New York. You can smell it. The ginkgo trees were dropping their yellow nuts and blanketing the ground, stinking like rancid butter. This offensive smell is an annual fall event. *(WALL STREET JOURNAL, 12November2021)*

SMELL: LIKE SMELL OF DECAYING VEGETATION: (THING) ... they smelled the raw odor of decaying river vegetation, so unlike the faintly musty smell of the forest. *(THE SKY AND THE FOREST by C. S. Foreste)*

SMELL: LIKE WOLF'S MUSK ODOR: (THING) The very odor on the man was wild, a strong meaty reek, like a wolf's musk. *(THE LIVING REED by Pearl S. Buck)*

SMILE: LIKE CHESHIRE CAT: (PERSON) ... smiled like a Cheshire cat. (Author)

SMILE: LIKE NEGOTIATING WALK: (PERSON) ...pasted a smile on her face and dragged herself toward the ... like a woman negotiating a walk down death row. *(JEWELS OF THE SUN by Nora Roberts)*

SNAP: LIKE RUBBER BAND: (PERSON) was fighting so hard to push him out, using all her strength, that when she finally did—it was like a rubber band snapping. *(FEAR THE DARK by Kay Hooper)*

SNAP: LIKE STRETCHED RUBBER BAND: (PERSON) She had a smile that snapped back like a stretched rubber band. (Readers Digest *TOWARD MORE PICTURESQUE SPEECH*)

SNAPPED: LIKE TOYS: AIRCRAFT: (THING) A half-dozen aircraft still on the flight-line would never leave it, their wings snapped like toys from the blast of a missile that had exploded directly over the runway crossroads. *(RED STORM RISING by Tom Clancy)*

SNARL: LIKE WILDCAT: (PERSON) she snarled at him like a wildcat. *(CIRCLE OF FATE by Charlotte Lamb)*

SNEAK: LIKE SHADOW: CAT: (THING) "The gray cat snuck away toward the open barn shed and passed inside like a shadow." *(THE GRAPES OF WRATH by John Steinbeck)*

SNIFF AIR: LIKE HOUND SEEKING SCENT: (THING) He stopped momentarily, sniffed the air like a hound seeking some fugitive scent, then kicked the snow off his boots and struck off up the hill at a tangent. (*THE GUNS OF NAVORONE* by Alistair Maclean)

SNIFF: LIKE SOMEONE TASTING BAD EGG: (THING) A peculiar stagnant smell hung over the anchorage—a smell of sodden leaves and rotting tree trunks. The doctor was sniffing and sniffing, like someone tasting a bad egg. (*TREASURE ISLAND* by Robert Louis Stevenson)

SNIFF: LIKE STUFFING BLOW FLY UP NOSE: (PERSON) Sniffing coke is like stuffing a blow fly up your nose. (Unknown)

SNOW FALLING: LIKE STORM OF ARCHES: (THING) Snow...fell like a storm of arches from a coldly burning sky. (Unknown)

SNOW FLAKES DESCENDING: LIKE WET ASTERISKS: (THING) ... flakes descending like large, wet asterisks. (Unknown)

SNOW VANISHING: LIKE GHOSTLY PERFORMERS IN WIND: (THING) Snow drove relentlessly through the yellow cones of the headlights. Now and then, when the wind faltered or briefly changed the angle of its assault, short-lived forms of snow capered in arabesque dances, this way and that, but always dispersing and vanishing like ghostly performers the moment that the wind recovered its momentum and purpose. (Unknown)

SNOW-FILLED SKY: LOOKED LIKE SLAB OF DARK-GRAY GRANITE: (THING) It was snowing...the sky looked like a great slab of dark-gray granite. (*STRANGERS* by Dean R. Koontz)

SNUGGLE: LIKE KITTEN: (PERSON) The two girls rushed to the fireplace joyfully, holding out their chilled hands to the blaze, snuggling to its warmth like two half-frozen kittens. (*THE RADIO BOYS AT MOUNTAIN PASS* by Allen Chapman)

SOFT AND ROUNDED: LIKE WOMAN: MOUNTAIN: (PLACE) The road ran straight toward the little foothills on the first mountain range—rounded, woman-like hills, soft and sexual as flesh. (*THE WAYWARD BUS* by John Steinbeck)

SOFT WHITE: LIKE DOLL HOUSE: HOUSE: (PLACE) It was like a doll's house, all soft white with forest-green trim, the many paned windows flanked by shutters that looked functional as well as decorative. The roof was thatched, a charming wonder. A wind chime made up of three columns of bells sang musically. (*JEWELS OF THE SUN* by Nora Roberts)

SOUND OF CLUBBING: LIKE CHOPPING DOWN TREE: (PERSON) He recalled when he brought in a large fish too green and it nearly tore his boat to pieces—it's tail slapping and banging and breaking the thwart—and the sound of the clubbing of it like chopping a tree down. (*RECKONING* by Catherine Coulter)

SOUND OF SHOTS: LIKE FIRECRACKERS: (PERSON) Shots rang out like firecrackers along the shore by trigger-happy hunters shooting fish. (*Wall Street Journal* 2May1988)

SOUND OF SILENCE: LIKE A SOFT AND HUSHED SNOWFALL: (THING) The silence was like a gentle snowfall, soft and hushed, as soothing as the whisper of a summer wind, as quiet as the passage of stars. (*THE SANDS OF TIME* by Sidney Sheldon)

SOUND STOOD OUT: LIKE PROVERBIAL SORE THUMB: (THING) The one meaningful sound among it all, stood out like the proverbial sore thumb from the rest. (Unknown)

SOUND: CRACK: LIKE CANNON:: (THING) The canvas cracked like cannon and the blocks trundled and banged on the deck as the ship continued to drift away, not only with the speed of the current, but by the whole amount of her leeway. (*TREASURE ISLAND* by Robert Louis Stevenson)

SOUND: CRUNCH: LIKE DRIED CEREAL: FOREST: (PLACE) It was an early autumn morning and a frosty chill hung in the air. The sweet surrendering scent of the morning dew filled the forest with a scent that did not belong on earth. Autumn leaves from the tall trees lay scattered on the forest floor; each of them turning brittle brown; there was a sound like dried cereal being crunched underfoot, pushing their papery remains deep into the soft soil. The dark shadows of the voluminous trees and the surrounding bushes had become the backbone of the forest, standing as passive protectors of a peaceful place. The autumn sun rose in a hurry as if trying to make up for setting too early the evening before, blooming into the pale sky with a warm mellow glow, sending what was left of the moon packing until its next shift guarding the night. By mid-morning the sky was a brilliant baby blue. As the morning developed the sound of young birds filled the air chirping, tweeting and warbling incessantly. (Unknown)

SOUND: LIKE AN APOLOGY: (THING) ... it sounds in my ears like an apology. *(THE WINTER OF OUR DISCONTENT* by John Steinbeck*)*

SOUND: LIKE CAR BRAKING HARD: (THING) The war-shot on the deep submarine created an awful sound—the sudden pressure change as the pressure hull was penetrated, rushing air, and then a horrible screech—like a car braking hard—as the bulkheads caved in—then the sound of the hull collapsing, hollow boom, sort of. And that's it: over a hundred people dead. (*RED STORM RISING* by Tom Clancy)

SOUND: LIKE FREIGHT TRAIN: CAT: (THING) A lean black cat was stretched out on the sidewalk staring out of golden eyes at people passing by. When people stopped to scratch between its ears, it narrowed its eyes and let out a purr that sounded like a freight train. (*JEWELS OF THE SUN* by Nora Roberts*)*

SOUND: LIKE GHOSTS: (THING) The figures looked strange and unnatural against the snowy deck; their feet made no as they moved over the deck. They were like ghosts in their noiselessness, treading the thick carpet of snow. (*THE CAPTAIN FROM CONNECTICUT* by C.S. Forester)

SOUND: LIKE GOD SNAPPING HIS FINGERS: (THING) If the surface retains much of the light, the heat energy from the laser could blast the coating right off the glass, then blow the meter apart. He watched a half-meter mirror let go once. It sounded like God snapping His fingers. (*THE CARDINAL OF THE KREMLIN* by Tom Clancy)

SOUND: LIKE GROWLING AND BARKING AND GRUNTING: (THING) ... sounds like growling and barking and grunting, punctuated at times by shrill screams. (*TARZAN AT THE EARTH'S CORE* by Edgar Rice Burroughs)

SOUND: LIKE INVERTED CUP: DONKEY: (THING) He was petted and loved and spoken to. On the tether, he watched Mary go about her duties. He flicked the flies from his hears and sometimes, when he tired of watching, his eyes closed and he locked his knees to that he would not fall, and he slept standing up. He was not a stubborn animal. He was most patient and he would stand while Joseph burdened him with a mound of objects. When the bridle strap was pulled by his master, the ass lowered his head, switched his tail against his flanks, and started off, the little hoofs making sounds like an inverted cup dropped in the mud. (*THE DAY CHRIST WAS BORN* by Jim Bishop)

SOUND: LIKE MUFFLED BELL: (THING) It rang like a muffled bell. (Unknown)

SOUND: LIKE OLD PENITENT SONG: (THING) The sound of the cattle in the pens lowing for their calves day and night haunted her. It had a regular rhythmic beat like the old Penitent songs...it was loud and raw under the stars in that wide empty country. (*INSIGHT* Article by Jane Addams Allen)

SOUND: LIKE PEACOCK: STORE: (PLACE) "Along 66 the hamburger stands. Board-and-bat shacks. There were two gasoline pumps in front, a screen door, a long bar, stools, and a foot rail. Near the door three slot machines, showing through glass the wealth in nickels three bars will bring. And beside them, the nickel phonograph with records piled up like pies, ready to swing out to the turntable and play dance music. "Ti-pi-ti-pi-tin," "Thanks for the Memory," Bing Crosby, Benny Goodman. At one end of the counter a covered case;

candy cough drops, caffeine sulphate called Sleepless, No-Doze; candy, cigarettes, razor blades, aspirin, Brome-Seltzer, Alka-Seltzer. The walls decorated with posters, bathing girls, blondes with big breasts and slender hips and waxen faces, in white bathing suits, and holding a bottle of Coca-Cola and smiling—see what you get with a Coca-Cola. Long bar, and salts, peppers, mustard pots, and paper napkins. Beer taps behind the counter, and in back the coffee urns, shiny and steaming, with glass gauges showing the coffee level. And [there were] pies in wire cages and oranges in pyramids of four. And little piles of Post Toasties, corn flakes, stacked up in designs. The signs on cards, picked out with shining mica: Pies Like Mother Used to Make. Credit Makes Enemies, Let's Be Friends. Ladies May Smoke But Be Careful Where You Lay Your Butts. Eat Here and Keep Your Wife for a Pet. Down at one end the cooking plates, pots of stew, potatoes, pot roast, roast beef, gray roast pork waiting to be sliced. Minnie or Susy or Mae, middle-aging behind the counter, hair curled and rouge and powder [applied] on a sweating face; taking orders in a soft low voice, calling them out to the cook with a screech like a peacock; mopping the counter with circular strokes, polishing the big shining coffee urns. The cook is Joe or Carl or Al, hot in a white coat and apron, beady sweat on white forehead, below the white cook's cap, moody, rarely speaking, looking up for a moment at each new entry. Wiping the griddle, slapping down the hamburger. He repeats Mae's orders gently, scrapes the griddle, and wipes it down with burlap. Moody and silent."
(THE GRAPES OF WRATH by John Steinbeck)

    SOUND: LIKE PISTOL SHOT: (THING) It sounded like a pistol shot far away to the north. (*WINTER SUNLIGHT* by Susan Alexander)

    SOUND: LIKE RIPPING LINEN:: (THING) Fired from behind another hill three kilometers away, the shells arced through the sky to their left, cutting through the air with a sound like the ripping of linen. (*RED STORM RISING* by Tom Clancy)

SOUND: LIKE SINGING: (PERSON) When he spoke English, it sounded like he was nearly singing, kind of like Andrea Bocelli. (*RECKONING* by Catherine Coulter)

SPARKLED LIKE: HAND: (PERSON) [As she] walked toward him and held out a hand, [he noticed] her hand was long and narrow. Rings sparkled on it like jewels on white silk. He was afraid to squeeze too hard. (*HEAVEN AND EARTH* by Nora Roberts)

SPAWN: LIKE A FILM: (THING) Memory's a spawner. Start with one clear detailed print, and it springs into action and it can go forward or back like a film, once it starts. *(THE WINTER OF OUR DISCONTENT* by John Steinbeck*)*

SPEAK WORDS: LIKE SEPARATE TILES: (PERSON) Although he spoke in parables, they laid his words down like separate tiles and took them literally. (*MIDNIGHT SHADOWS* by Nora Roberts)

SPEAK WORDS: LIKE SUN SHINING ON POND: (PERSON) His words were like the sun shining on a pond until the water evaporates and becomes clouds of rain. He moved an entire block of "MAGA" voters. (Dick Morris March 5, 2024)

SPEAK: LIKE SLAP IN FACE: (PERSON) his words were like a slap in the face. (*CIRCLE OF FATE* by Charlotte Lamb)

SPILL DOWN: LIKE SUNLIGHT: (PERSON) The boy's joyful laugh spilled down like sunlight. (*THE BECOMING* by Nora Roberts)

SPIN THROUGH MIND: LIKE FILM RUNNING AT INSANE SPEED: (THING) the day seemed to spin crazily through her mind, like a film being run at insane speed. (*HEARTLAND* by Bethany Campbell)

SPIN: LIKE LITTLE GIRL: (THING) The leaves scud over the ground and take small flights into the air. As I toss my head back and raise my eyes to the sky a smile spreads from freckled cheek to cheek. The branches sway like the arms of a soccer crowd and in their chaotic dance they are hypnotically beautiful. My mind relaxes and I feel the happiness of my life bubble up from within. The light I keep inside begins to escape from my pores. Were it not for the "passers by" I would spin like a little girl again, arms out wide and fingers spread, but instead I keep my hands in my pockets and inhale deeply. This wind carries the fragrance of the woodland, the essence of my childhood days... (Unknown)

SPIN: LIKE PLUMB-BOB: (PERSON) He swung head downward, spinning dizzily like a human plumb-bob. (*TARZAN AT THE EARTH'S CORE* by Edgar Rice Burroughs)

SPIRAL DOWN: LIKE SEEDPOD FROM TREE: (THING) The missile had sizable negative buoyancy, and the added mass in the nose tipped it over. The nose-heavy trim gave it an eccentric path, and it spiraled down like a seedpod from a tree. *(THE HUNT FOR RED OCTOBER* by Tom Clancy)

SPIT OUT: LIKE GNAT: (PERSON) "The Russian people will always be able to distinguish true patriots from scum and traitors and will simply spit them out like a gnat that accidentally flew into their mouths. (President Putin on national TV *THE NEW YORK SUN* article by James Brooke)

SPOON: LIKE CHICKEN SOUP: (PERSON) She spooned up what smelled like chicken soup. (*ABANDONED IN DEATH* by J. D. Robb)

SPRAY: LIKE PHLEGM: (PERSON) ... spittle sprayed out like phlegm from an excited boy's mouth. (Author)

SPREAD DEATH: LIKE POISONED CLOUD: CONTACTS: (THING) The world ended with bangs and whimpers, with blood and pain, with fear and dread. A cashier handing change to a customer, a mother nursing her child, businessmen gripping hands over a deal—these and so many simple contacts spread death like a poisoned cloud over the world. (*THE RISE OF MAGICKS* by Nora Roberts)

SPREAD: LIKE FIRE: (PERSON) Electric tension spread like fire between them. They were watching each other across the width of his study, like fencers waiting for the signal to engage. (*LOVE UPON THE WIND* by Sally Stewart)

SPREAD: ACTION: SPIN: (PERSON) In a mad dance, she spin across the sand, above it, her arms spread like wings, her hair falling in coils, like snakes. (*HEAVEN AND EARTH* by Nora Roberts)

SPREAD: LIKE MUCUS: (PERSON) People who have a firm repulsion to anything [fill in the blank] they eat this stuff up, and arrogantly spread lies and untruths around like mucus on a baby's bib. (Comment posted online)

SPREAD: LIKE QUILT: EARTH: (PLACE) she watched from the plane window as the hills and mountains of the east fell behind and the earth below her turned flat. Beneath her, the plains spread like a giant's crazy quilt in vivid shades of green, where only an occasional river stretched out, thin as an errant thread. (*HEARTLAND* by Bethany Campbell)

SPREAD: LIKE SECRETARY'S BACKSIDE: (PERSON) "Million people marching together, disease will spread like a secretary's backside." (Unknown)

SPREAD: LIKE WILDFIRE: (THING) The news would soon spread ... like a wildfire. (*LOVE UPON THE WIND* by Sally Stewart)

SPRING: LIKE NEW VOLCANO: (THING) The war seemed to be springing from the ground like a new volcano. (*RED STORM RISING* by Tom Clancy)

SPRING: LIKE THISTLES IN WEED PATCH: (THING) Troubles sprang up like thistles in a weed patch. (Unknown)

SPROUT: LIKE WEEDS: (PERSON) They were people who got excited about new things and unconsciously sought the synergism that made ideas sprout like weeds in the disordered garden of the laboratory. (*THE CARDINAL OF THE KREMLIN* by Tom Clancy)

SPURT: LIKE MUD: ROAD: (PLACE) The old road was simply a slice of country, uncultivated to start, marked only by wheel ruts and pounded by horses' hoofs. In the summer a heavy cloud of dust arose from its surface when a wagon went by, and in winter, paste-like mud spurted from under horses' feet. Gradually the road became scooped out so that it was lower than the fields through which it traveled, and this made it a long lake of standing water in the winter, sometimes very deep. (*THE DAY CHRIST WAS BORN* by Jim Bishop)

SQUIRM: LIKE CAUGHT RABBIT: (PERSON) ... squirmed like a rabbit caught in a noose. (Author)

SQUIRM: LIKE DISCIPLINED CHILD: (PERSON) ... squirmed like a child being disciplined. (Author)

SQUIRM: LIKE HOOKED WORM: (PERSON) ... squirmed like a worm on a hook. (Author)

SQUIRM: LIKE LYING CHILD: (PERSON) ... squirmed like a child caught in a lie. (Author)

SQUIRM: LIKE ROPED STEER: (PERSON) ... squirmed like a roped steer. (Author)

SQUIRM: LIKE SNAKES: (PERSON) His doctor had read his blood pressure and told him to take it easy. Sitting in his office two weeks later, he felt an electric flash in his head behind his eyes, a feeling like a blinding blue-white glare for a second, and then he couldn't read anymore. It wasn't that he couldn't see. He saw clearly enough, but the words on a page swam and ran together and squirmed like snakes, and he couldn't make out what they said. He knew he had had a stroke. (*THE WAYWARD BUS* by John Steinbeck)

STALK OFF: LIKE OFFENDED DOWAGERS: DOG: (THING) the dog gulped down everything in his line of sight. The cats eyed him with disgust as he almost drained the water, wetting his ears profusely, and when he shook himself, they stalked off like offended dowagers, leaving him in clear possession of the field. (*COUNTRY OF THE HEART* by Robyn Donald)

STALK: LIKE RABID WOLF: (THING) The ship was stalking them to the east like a rabid wolf. He was not in an attractive position. (*Tom Clancy, THE HUNT FOR RED OCTOBER*)

STAND ALONG SIDE: LIKE SUCKLING CALVES: ROOM: (PLACE) I walked into his frosty den and he closed the door so softly that I did not hear the latch click. His desk was topped with plate glass, under which were lists of typed numbers. Two customers' chairs in echelon stood by his tall chair like twin suckling calves. They were comfortable but lower than the desk chair. When I sat down I had to look up and that put me in the position of supplication. (*THE WINTER OF OUR DISCONTENT* by John Steinbeck)

STAND OUT: LIKE SHINY WAVES: (PERSON) He noticed the sun glinting off the waves far below, standing out like shiny blue furrows. (*PATRIOT GAMES* by Tom Clancy)

STAND: LIKE DISRUPTIVE SCHOOLKIDS: (PERSON) … was standing behind her desk in the richly paneled office when they entered, her arms crossed over her gray, Armani-suited chest. She said nothing at all until the three of them were standing directly in front of her desk, like disruptive schoolkids in front of a head master to be disciplined. Behind her impressive desk was a wall of solid built-in wooden bookcases filled to overflowing with books and knickknacks and a dozen shining photographic moments with various heads of state. It wasn't an overly-large office, small enough to be fitting for a servant of the people. But still, it announced power, tradition, and a big fist. (*POWER PLAY* by Catherine Coulter)

STAND: LIKE STONE: (PERSON) He stood like stone, his eyes fixed on the path. (*THE LIVING REED* by Pearl S. Buck)

STAND: LIKE TOMBSTONES: (PERSON) They could see that the area was not good for seclusion. The sparse trees were bare of leaves, and the apartment buildings stood like tombstones on flat, open land. (*THE CARDINAL OF THE KREMLIN* by Tom Clancy)

STANDING TREES: LIKE CANDLES OF YELLOW FLAME: (THING) Against the gray cliffs of the mountains tall narrow poplar trees rose like candles of yellow flame standing single and emphatic. *(THE LIVING REED* by Pearl S. Buck*)*

STANDING TRUMPET: LIKE GOLDEN LILIES: (THING) Ahead of her were huge trumpets standing on end, their wide mouths looking like golden lilies against the marble of the temple. (*THE DAY CHRIST WAS BORN* by Jim Bishop)

STANDING: LIKE GHOSTS IN TWILIGHT: FOREST: (PLACE) Under an open sky with the chance of an unimpeded breeze, the gloomy forest, with the tree trunks standing like ghosts in the twilight oppressed him ... He hated this forest, with its darkness and silence. *(THE SKY AND THE FOREST* by C. S. Forester*)*

STANDING: LIKE SPIKES: TOWN: (PLACE) Rustic cabins dotted the grassy hills as trees stood up like spikes, zig-zagging the border of brick roads and unpolished homes. Rivers streamed through deep valleys. (Unknown)

STARING FACES: LIKE EGGS IN CRATE: (PERSON) The faces, like so many evenly spaced eggs in a crate and just as neutral in expression, stared up at him. (*THE DAY CHRIST DIED* by Jim Bishop)

STARING: LOOKED LIKE EYES: FOREST: (PLACE) The woodland seemed ominously quiet. They paused, now that even the sound of their own footfalls was silent, all that could be heard was the susurration of the leaves in the gusty wind. Looking up, they were transfixed by the myriad of fluttering leaves that danced in the high boughs, making a living roof above them. They were calmed, almost hypnotized, but the longer they stared the more the leaves looked like eyes staring back down at them and the boughs seemed to draw closer, blocking the sunlight as if they were forming a cage around them. (Unknown)

STARS AT SEA: LIKE GEMSTONES ON VELVET SHEET: (THING) The night was calm and clear, the sort of sky you get only at sea, ablaze with stars, like gemstones on a velvet sheet. (*THE CARDINAL OF THE KREMLIN* by Tom Clancy)

STARS BLAZING: LIKE JEWELS ON BLACK VELVET: (THING) at night the clear sky expanded with stars blazing like jewels on black velvet. (*PATRIOT GAMES* by Tom Clancy)

STERN: LIKE JUDGE: (PERSON) He was a beautiful man, all tough-looking and stern like a judge, until he smiled and a dark eyebrow shot up in question. (*RECKONING* by Catherine Coulter)

STICK TO: LIKE FLIES ON FLYPAPER: (THING) "I use ta think that'd cut 'er," he said. "Use ta rip off a prayer an' all the troubles'd stick to that prayer like flies on flypaper, an' the prayer'd go a-sailin' off, a-takin' them troubles along." (*THE GRAPES OF WRATH* by John Steinbeck)

STICK TO: LIKE SECOND SKIN: (PERSON) "I have an FBI agent sticking to me like a second skin." (*POWER PLAY* by Catherine Coulter)

STILL GREY EYES: MALE: RIDER: (PERSON) The other rider was a cowboy, young in years, with still gray eyes like Miss Preston's, and [with an] intent, expressionless face, dark from sun and wind. (*SUNSET PASS* by Zane Grey)

STING: LIKE SMALL BITTER FIRES: JELLYFISH: (THING) The summer sea was crowded with little jellyfish the size of gooseberries, dangling their tendrils and their nettle cells. As they washed in against my legs and belly I felt the sting like small bitter fires, and the slow wave breathed in and out. (*THE WINTER OF OUR DISCONTENT* by John *Steinbeck*)

STOMP: ACTION: BREATHE: (PERSON) Hissing out a breath, she backtracked, then came back up on the porch stomping like a horse and whistling. (*HEAVEN AND EARTH* by Nora Roberts)

STOOD OUT: MALE: RIDER: (PERSON) He dismounted and was partly drunk; that was not the striking thing about him. He looked and breathed the very spirit of the range at its wildest. He was tall, lean and lithe, with a handsome red face, like a devil's eyes, hot as blue flame, and yellow hair that curled scraggily from under a dusty black sombrero. He had just been clean-shaved. Drops of blood and sweat stood out like beads on his lean jowls and curved lips. A gun swung below his hip. (*SUNSET PASS* by Zane Grey)

STOP: LIKE STAMPING ON COCKROACH: (PERSON) He regarded stopping the bad person as an act of virtue, like stamping on a cockroach. (*TREASURE ISLAND* by Robert Louis Stevenson)

STORE: LIKE SQUIRREL: (PERSON) She stored her money away like a squirrel its nuts. When she had enough to content her, she'd be off. (*JEWELS OF THE SUN by Nora Roberts*)

STRAIN: LIKE ELEPHANT LEGS: TURTLE: THING:... over the grass at the roadside a land turtle crawled, turning aside for nothing, dragging his high-domed shell over the grass. His hard legs and yellow-nailed feet threshed slowly through the grass, not really walking, but boosting and dragging his shell along. The barley beads slid off his shell, and the clover burrs fell on him and rolled to the ground. His horny beak was partly open, and his fierce, humorous eyes, under brows like fingernails, stared straight ahead. He came over the grass leaving a beaten trail behind him, and the hill, which was the highway embankment, reared up ahead of him. For a moment he stopped, his head held high. He blinked and looked up and down. At last he started to climb the embankment. Front clawed feet reached forward but did not touch. The hind feet kicked his shell along, and it scraped on the grass, and on the gravel. As the embankment grew steeper and steeper, the more frantic were the efforts of the land turtle. Pushing hind legs strained and slipped, boosting the shell along, and the horny head protruded as far as the neck could stretch. Little by little the shell slid up the embankment until at last a parapet cut straight across its line of march, the shoulder of the road, a concrete wall four inches high. As though they worked independently the hind legs pushed the shell against the wall. The head upraised and peered over the wall to the broad smooth plain of cement. Now the hands raced on top of the wall, strained and lifted, and the shell came slowly up and rested its front end on the wall. For a moment the turtle rested. A red ant ran into the shell, into the soft skin inside the shell, and suddenly head and legs snapped in, and the armored tail clamped in sideways. The red ant was crushed between body and legs. And one head of wild oats was clamped into the shell by a front leg. For a long moment the turtle lay still, and then the neck crept out and the old humorous frowning eyes looked about and the legs and tail came out. The back legs went to work, straining like elephant legs, and the shell tipped to an angle so that the front legs could not reach the level cement plain. But higher and higher the hind legs boosted it, until at last the center of balance was reached, the front tipped down, the front legs scratched at the pavement, and it was up. But the head of wild oats was held by its stem around the front legs. - Now the going was easy, and all the legs worked, and the shell boosted along, waggling from side to side. ... now it hurried on, for the highway was burning hot. A light truck approached, and as it came near, the driver saw the turtle and swerved to hit it. His front wheel struck the edge of the shell, flipped the turtle like a tidily-wink, spun it like a coin, and rolled it off the highway. The truck went back to its course along the right side. Lying on its back, the turtle was tight in its shell for a long time. But at last its legs waved in the air, reaching for something to pull it over. Its front foot caught a piece of quartz and little by little the shell pulled over and flopped upright. The wild oat head fell out and three of the spearhead seeds stuck in the ground. And as the turtle crawled on down the embankment, its shell dragged dirt over the seeds. The turtle entered a dirt road and jerked itself along, drawing a wavy shallow trench in the dust with its shell. The old humorous eyes looked ahead, and the horny beak opened a little. His yellow toe nails slipped a fraction in the dust. *(THE GRAPES OF WRATH* by John Steinbeck)

STREAM: LIKE PURE SUNLIGHT: FOREST: (PLACE) The woodland is like a droplet of paradise. The air is still, only the laughter of children in a nearby park reminds me that I'm still in the city. Here my dog can run free for hours and I can stop to watch nature. The sunlight streams in like it is more pure than the light I feel downtown, white, yet liquid gold at the same time. Nearby, on a rotting spindly tree, is a woodpecker hunting for insects, its brilliant red crest rocking back and forth as it pecks. Tiny chunks of wood fall to the leaf litter below, the sound dissipating into the woodland around. (Unknown)

STREAMING BACK: FEMALE: WITCH: (PERSON) Slender, with her cloak streaming back like bird-wings, she stood alone on the wind-whipped beach. Alone but for her rage and her grief; and her power; it was that power that filled her now, rushed inside her in wild pounding stroked like a lover gone mad. (*HEAVEN AND EARTH* by Nora Roberts)

STRETCH: LIKE COBWEBS: (THING) Silicon interconnects stretched like cobwebs across the wafer. (Author)

STRETCH: LIKE GIANT SHOE BOX: HOUSE: (PLACE) The house was long and narrow, perhaps only twelve feet wide at the front, but it stretched some thirty feet back like a giant shoe box. It was two stories high and had a one story extension at the rear for the kitchen. The wooden framed sash windows were propped open with sticks and the brick work, perhaps once a jaunty yellow, looked dirty with over a hundred years of London grime. A small rose garden had been planted in front, and although it had obviously once been carefully planned and loved, it was now riddled with weeds. (Unknown)

STRETCH: LIKE SPIDER LEGS: (THING) A guitar is … precious. I must learn this thing [unlike a harmonica]. Fingers of the left hand must have callus caps. Thumb of the right hand a horn of callus. Stretch the left-hand fingers stretch them like a spider's legs to get the hard pads on the frets. *(THE GRAPES OF WRATH* by John Steinbeck*)*

STRIKE: LIKE ANGRY PROTESTER: (PERSON) ... hit him like an angry protester. (Author)

STRIP OF PAVEMENT: LIKE RIBBON: ROAD: (PLACE) A red letter box stood as if on sentry duty, guarding the narrow exit to the Edwardian London no-through-road. The street was barely wide enough for two cars to pass in opposite directions and when people parked with wheels up on the ribbon-like strip of pavement, it was an obstacle course for pedestrians and drivers alike. (Unknown)

STROKE CHEEK: LIKE INDULGENT MOTHER: (PERSON) She stroked the boot like an indulgent mother her child's cheek. Her face was stunning and filled with sheer female delight. (*JEWELS OF THE SUN* by Nora Roberts)

STRONG: LIKE UNBREAKABLE TREE: (PERSON) strong—like a fragile tree that would bend but never break. (*QUINN* by Iris Johansen)

STUDY: LIKE SMEAR ON MICROSCOPE SLIDE: (PERSON) He studied her like something smeared on a slide and under a microscope. (*ABANDONED IN DEATH* by J. D. Robb)

SUCK INTO: LIKE TORNADO: (PERSON) I hoped I'd have more control, but it was like being sucked into a tornado. (Source *FINAL TARGET* by Iris Johansen)

SUN MELTED AWAY MIST: LIKE DEFROSTER ON CAR WINDOW: (THING) the sun melted away the morning mist like a defroster on a car window. (Unknown)

SUN STARED THROUGH WINDOW: LIKE ACCUSING EYE: (THING) The days were getting longer, and now the sun didn't shine in her face when she drove to work. Instead it stared right through her bedroom window like an accusing eye. (*THE CARDINAL OF THE KREMLIN* by Tom Clancy)

SUN STRUCK FACE: LIKE A BLESSING: (THING) The sun struck her face like a blessing, and she stopped and closed her eyes. "Isn't it beautiful today? And smell that grass. I love mornings after a rain." *(FINAL TARGET* by Iris Johansen*)*

SUPPORT LIFE: LIVE LIKE BIRD: FOOD: (THING) There is food to be found in the forest, enough to support life if one is content to live like a bird, not from day to day but from hour to hour, with almost every waking moment devoted to the search. ... all to be noted by a sharp eye when wandering in the forest. *(THE SKY AND THE FOREST* by *C. S. Forrester)*

SUPPORT: LIKE UPSIDE-DOWN BOWL: (THING) The leather hatbox was open on the floor. It had a support made of velvet-covered cardboard like an upside-down porridge bowl. *(THE WINTER OF OUR DISCONTENT* by John Steinbeck*)*

SWALLOW: LOOKED LIKE SNAKE: AIRCRAFT: (THING) The aircraft was little more than a platform of a large, infrared telescope that could be made to fit in the wide-bodied airliner. The engineers had given the fuselage an ungainly humpback immediately aft of the flight deck that extended half its length, and the 767 looked like a snake that had just swallowed something large enough to shock on. *(THE CARDINAL OF THE KREMLIN* by Tom Clancy*)*

SWAT: LIKE INTRUSIVE FLY: (PERSON) ... swatted the thought from her mind like an intrusive fly. *(LOVE UPON THE WIND* by Sally Stewart*)*

SWAYING BRANCHES: LIKE ARMS OF SOCCER CROWD: FOREST: (PLACE) The leaves scud over the ground and take small flights into the air. As I toss my head back and raise my eyes to the sky a smile spreads from freckled cheek to cheek. The branches sway like the arms of a soccer crowd and in their chaotic dance they are hypnotically beautiful. My mind relaxes and I feel the happiness of my life bubble up from within. The light I keep inside begins to escape from my pores. Were it not for those passing by I would spin like a little girl again, arms out wide and fingers spread, but instead I keep my hands in my pockets and inhale deeply. This wind carries the fragrance of the woodland, the essence of my childhood days... (Unknown)

SWEAT: ACTION: (PERSON) His stomach tightened into sweaty fists, and the heat slicked his body like a second skin. (*NIGHTWORK* by Nora Roberts)

SWEAT: LIKE RIVER: (PERSON) Chills racked her so her teeth clacked together; when it passed, sweat poured and ran down her body like a river. (*ABANDONED IN DEATH* by J. D. Robb)

SWEET TOOTH: LIKE OVERINDULGED CHILD: (PERSON) As a child I hunted and killed small creatures with energy and joy. Rabbits and squirrels, small birds, and later ducks and wild geese came crashing down, rumpled distortions of bone and blood and fur and feathers. There was a savage creativeness about it without hatred or rancor or guilt. The war retired my appetite for destruction; perhaps I was like a child overindulged in sweets. A shotgun's blast was no longer a shout of fierce happiness. [I no longer found joy in killing.] (*THE WINTER OF OUR DISCONTENT* by John Steinbeck)

SWEET: LIKE BROTHER: (PERSON) That stopped her in her tracks. "Day is not an idiot. He's sweet, like a brother to me. He saw the lie perching on the end of her nose. (*POWER PLAY* by Catherine Coulter)

SWELLING EYE: LIKE CHICKPEA: (PERSON) His ear swelled like a chickpea. (Unknown)

SWOLLEN: LIKE TRAFFIC JAM: (THING) the nerves were so swollen that the nerve tunnels were like a traffic jam. (*HEARTLAND* by Bethany)

TACKLE: LIKE FOOTBALL PLAYER: (PERSON) Like a football player, he launched himself through the air; his long arms encircled the legs of the fleeing native, bringing him heavily to the ground. (*TARZAN AT THE EARTH'S CORE* by Edgar Rice Burroughs)

TACKY: LIKE FLESH: (THING) The talisman was a kind of mound of translucent stone, four inches in diameter and an inch and a half at its rounded peak. Carved on its surface was an endless interweaving shape that seemed to move and yet went no place. It was living, but had no head or tail, nor beginning or end. The polished stone was not slick to the touch but slightly tacky like flesh, and it was always warm to the touch. You could see into it and yet not through it. Its color and convolutions and texture changed as my needs changed. *(THE WINTER OF OUR DISCONTENT* by John Steinbeck)

TAKE IN: LIKE WATER: (PERSON) ... gulping in all the sights like water. (THE BECOMING by Nora Roberts)

TAKEN OVER: LIKE BUNCH OF PUPPETS: (THING) Taken over like a bunch of puppets. (Unknown)

TAN RAINCOATS: LOOK ALIKE: (THING) An old cotton raincoat—all tan cotton raincoats look alike—and a pair of those clear tear-off cellophane gloves that come on a roll. *(THE WINTER OF OUR DISCONTENT by John Steinbeck)*

TARGET: LIKE MOUSE WITH HAWK IN SKY ABOVE: (THING) It was like being a mouse, with a hawk above in the sky. (*THE CARDINAL OF THE KREMLIN* by Tom Clancy)

TASTE: LIKE SALTED CARDBOARD: (THING) ... tasted like salted cardboard. (*Unknown*)

TASTE: LIKE SPOILED EGG: (PERSON) Why did it revolt me and leave a taste like a spoiled egg? (*THE WINTER OF OUR DISCONTENT* by John Steinbeck)

TASTE: LIKE SUGAR-COATED BOOK COVER: (THING) ... tasted like a sugar-coated book cover. (*Unknown*)

TAX: LIKE STANDING IN BUCKET AND TRYING TO LIFT SELF: (THING) *"We contend that for a nation to tax itself into prosperity is like a man standing in a bucket and trying to lift himself by the handles."* – Winston Churchill

TERMINAL: LOOKED LIKE ALIEN SPACESHIP: AIRPORT: TERMINAL: (THING) The terminal looked like the alien spaceship in Spielberg's *Close Encounters* movie. (*THE CARDINAL OF THE KREMLIN* by Tom Clancy)

THEORY POPPED: LIKE SOAP BUBBLE: (THING) his 'theory' popped like a soap bubble when someone with more knowledge on the subject proved his assertion wrong (*QUORA* comment June 19, 2024)

THICK COBWEBS: LIKE HALLOWEEN: BASEMENT: (PLACE) The basement looked like something from a 1940s movie set. There were thick cobwebs everywhere, like Halloween had come early. (*RECKONING* by Catherine Coulter)

THICK FOG: LIKE DRIVING IN BALL OF COTTON: (THING) ... fog so thick, it was like driving in the middle of a ball of cotton. (*Unknown*)

THICK: LIKE HEAD STUFFED WITH COTTON: (PERSON) She was smiling, and surely that was a good sign. He didn't feel much of anything, no pain, and he wasn't about to test that out by moving. His head felt like it was stuffed with cotton—heavy and thick, with strange blurred thoughts that ricocheted here and there. He blinked, trying to clear his mind: it did, a bit. His mouth was so dry, but he couldn't say her name, but he tried—a small sound, but it got her attention. (*POWER PLAY* by Catherine Coulter)

THICKEN: LIKE DAY OLD STEW: TOWN: (PLACE) Under the unbroken cloud this late morning could be the pre-dawn and the street is all the more grey for it. The headache I woke with is thickening like day old stew. The cafe itself looks inviting, on the other side of those doors is warmth and soft jazz, but I have no time to pamper myself today. No money either. The coins that rattle in my pocket are all accounted for: bus fair, lunch and candy from the office vending machine at eleven. (*Unknown*)

THICKEN: LIKE FOG: (PERSON) ... constraint thickened like fog. (*LOVE UPON THE WIND* by Sally Stewart)

THICKEN: LIKE ONION: (THING) Like an onion, it grew larger as more coats were added to its thickness. The layers of new skin were then slowly unpeeled to reveal the treasure at the core. (Unknown)

THICKET: LIKE OAK TREES: WOODS: (PLACE) He came to a long thicket of oak-like trees—live, or evergreen oaks. I heard afterward they should be called—which grew along the sand like brambles, the boughs curiously twisted, the foliage compact, like thatch. The thicket stretched down from the top of one of the sandy knolls, spreading and growing taller as it went, until it reached the margin of the broad, reedy fen, through which the nearest of the little rivers soaked its way into the anchorage. The marsh was steaming in the strong sun, and the outline of the Spyglass trembled through the haze. (*TREASURE ISLAND* by Robert Louis Stevenson)

THIN: LIKE SKIN OVER LOOSE BONES: (PERSON) Maybe he worried about the dark circles that haunted her eyes, or how thin she felt—like skin over loose bones—when he hugged her, but her color was good, the eyes above those circles bright and happy. (*NIGHTWORK* by Nora Roberts)

THOUGHT OCCURRED: LIKE COLD CHILL: (THING) sometimes the thought came on him like a cold chill. (*HEARTLAND* by Bethany Campbell)

THREW DIRT: LIKE ROOSTER-TAIL FROM SPEEDBOAT: (THING) The tank's wide treads threw off dirt like the rooster-tail from a speedboat as it raced through the forest. (*RED STORM RISING* by Tom Clancy)

THRIFTY: LIKE FARMER ON MARKET DAY: (PERSON) He was like a farmer and his money on market day. He sought to find the best value he could before is money was expended. (*THE CAPTAIN FROM CONNECTICUT* by C.S. Forester)

THROW AROUND: LIKE MONOPOLY MONEY: (PERSON) Perhaps next time, he might want to consider the long-term economic implications before throwing around billions of dollars like Monopoly money. (Unknown)

THROW: LIKE POWDERED PAINT: FOREST: (PLACE) The woodland floor is a million hues of brown, more than Chloe's eyes can detect, yet they are there. The differences are magnified by the moisture, variation on variation. Mingled in are some stones, adding their greys to the mosaic beneath her feet. The trees are khaki over the bark, kissed with moss; on their shaded sides grows lichen as if thrown there like powdered paint, so softly green as to be close to white. (Unknown)

THUD SOUND: LIKE HEART BEAT: (THING) I sat down and turned out the light and sat listening to my house. It thudded like a heart, and maybe it was my heart and a rustling old house. *(THE WINTER OF OUR DISCONTENT by John Steinbeck)*

THUNDER CRASHED OVERHEAD: LIKE BALLS OF LEAD: (THING) Overhead, thunder crashed like balls of lead. *(JEWELS OF THE SUN by Nora Roberts)*

TOMBSTONE LINED UP: LIKE FALSE TEETH: (PLACE) A mirage belly-dances across the road leading to Styrofoam tombstones, arranged like false teeth in a ghastly smile. ("Color your Articles Sold" *THE WAYWARD BUS*)

TONE OF VOICE: LIKE SCAR ON CHEEK: (THING) Like the scar twisting whitely down his left cheek standing out more than usual now, his tone was an indication of an intensity of emotion he very, very rarely showed in any other way. *(FEAR THE DARK by Kay Hooper)*

TORN CLOUD HANGING: LIKE BLOODY RAG: (THING) "A large red drop of sun lingered on the horizon and then dripped over and was gone, and the sky was brilliant over the spot where it had gone, and a torn cloud, like a bloody rag, hung over the spot of its going. And dusk crept over the sky from the eastern horizon, and darkness crept over the land from the east. The evening star flashed and glittered in the dusk." *(THE GRAPES OF WRATH* by John Steinbeck*)*

TORNADO LOOPED AND WOBBLED: LIKE SPINNING TOP: (THING) The tornado looped and wobbled like a spinning top. (Author)

TOSS SOME(THING) LIKE SPITBALL: (PERSON) He tossed something like a spitball at me and it fell among the string beans. ... I picked up the green wad from the string beans—three twenty dollar bills folded in a tight square. (*THE WINTER OF OUR DISCONTENT* by John Steinbeck)

TREAT: LIKE A SON: (PERSON) Of the disciples, John was the one who was beloved of Jesus. He was treated like a son, who could almost always bring about a paternal smile of affection; one who could win concessions denied to others. Of all the apostles, the brothers, James and John, together with Peter were the closest to Jesus. John inherited some of the violence of his father, and once, when a Samaritan village spurned a visit from Jesus, John was in favor of calling down fire from heaven to consume the people of the village. (THE DAY CHRIST DIED by Jim Bishop)

TREATMENT: LIKE HOLDING DAUGHTER FOR CHILE ABUSE: (PERSON) Leukemia or cancer treatment is like standing by holding your daughter for child abuse. (Unknown)

TREES: LIKE PARK: COUNTRYSIDE: (PLACE) A mountain torrent tumbled along the center of the grassy floor. Giant trees grew at spaced intervals; lending a park-like appearance to the scene ... gorgeous blooms blossomed in the trees. (*TARZAN AT THE EARTH'S CORE* by Edgar Rice Burroughs)

TREMBLE: LIKE LEAF: (PERSON) He began to tremble like a leaf and for the first time realized the extent of the nervous strain he had been undergoing. (*TARZAN AT THE EARTH'S CORE* by Edgar Rice Burroughs)

THE METAPHORS OF LIKE 147

TROUBLE SPRING: LIKE THISTLES IN WEED PATCH: (THING) Troubles sprang up like thistles in a weed patch. (Unknown)

TWIRL AWAY: LIKE RELINQUISHED BATON: (PERSON) One of the attackers instantly fell before his stream of fire, plastic sabot rounds slamming into his chest, his weapon twirling out of his grasp like a relinquished baton. Another dropped down after him in a gush of sand. *(POWER PLAYS POLITIKA* by Tom Clancy and Martin Greenberg)

UNBAG: LIKE RUMPLED NEST: HARBOR: (PLACE) ... was flecked with summer craft, slim hulls with sails covered in grommeted coats of canvas, and here and there a morning man made ready, clearing boom and coiling jib- and mainsheets, unbagging his Genoa like a great white rumpled nest. *(THE WINTER OF OUR DISCONTENT by John Steinbeck)*

UNLOCKING SHIMS: NEEDLE-LIKE: (PERSON) She turned her flash onto the lock plate below the door knob. Then she produced a flat leather case from a patch pocket on her coveralls. Zipping open the case, she selected two needle-like steel shims from the large set inside, clamped one between her teeth, and inserted the working end of the other into the keyhole. She raked it deftly across the bottom cylinder pins, felt one, then two of them activate. Seconds later she extracted the pick from the keyway, switched it with the one in her mouth, and used the second to jiggle open the remaining tumblers. The latch slid back with a metallic *snick*. She twisted the doorknob, applied slight pressure to the door with her shoulder. It eased forward a crack. (*POWER PLAYS POLITIKA* by Tom Clancy and Martin Greenberg)

UNMARKED: NOT LIKE THAT NOW: ROAD: HIGHWAY: (PLACE) What do you think of our highway? I found these roads so different when I first came to Canada. They scared me with their two or three lanes in both directions - and it's just a regular road really. A decade ago a lot of them didn't even have "cats eyes," combine that with no streetlights and heavy rain in the dead of night and no-one slowing down... it isn't like that now though, in the spring sunshine it's a benign swathe of tired grey with white painted lines and for the most part quite straight. I guess it's like the English motorways I used to drive on, but here there are traffic lights since it connects different parts of the city. As long as the traffic doesn't snarl up they're pretty fast... (Unknown)

UNPEEL: LIKE ONION: (PERSON) Like an onion, it grew larger as more coats were added to its thickness. The layers of new skin were then slowly unpeeled to reveal the treasure at the core. (Unknown)

UNREEL FINAL DAY: LIKE MOTION PICTURE: (PERSON) He is a man who can recreate the final day in a life in infinite detail, so that it unreels like a motion picture. (*THE DAY CHRIST DIED* by Jim Bishop)

USURP: LIKE INVADER: (PERSON) seemed like an invader, a usurper. (*HEARTLAND* by Bethany Campbell)

VANISH: ACTION: SEE: (PERSON) She was glowing. A faint aura of light outlined her body, her face, the long coils of her hair. Her eyes were green as a cat's against the dark. And she watched him steadily, patiently. As he started toward her, a ripple of air shivered over him. The sand shifted under his feet. He saw a single tear, diamond bright, slide down her cheek. [Then] she vanished like smoke. (*HEAVEN AND EARTH* by Nora Roberts)

VANISH: LIKE MIST: (PERSON) His patience ran thin at the best of times, but vanished like mist in the sun when he became angry. (*THE BECOMING* by Nora Roberts)

VANISH: LIKE PUFF OF SMOKE: (THING) If you faced them, they'd vanish like a puff of smoke. (*FINAL TARGET* by Iris Johansen)

VANISH: LIKE SHADOW: (PERSON) Fear vanished like a shadow in the night. (Unknown)

VANISH: LIKE WRAITH: (PERSON) ... dropped silently to the ground and vanished wraithlike into the darkness and the snow. (*THE SECRET WAYS* by Alstair MacLean)

THE METAPHORS OF LIKE   149

VENTING SOUND: LIKE MILLION TOILETS BEING FLUSHED: (THING) The venting ballast tanks sounded like a million toilets being flushed at once. *(THE HUNT FOR RED OCTOBER* by Tom Clancy*)*

VERTICAL: LIKE SMALL BROOMSTICK: (THING) It was like a small broomstick sitting vertically in the water, about a mile away. As the waves rolled past, the bottommost visible part of the periscope flared out. *(*Tom Clancy, *THE HUNT FOR RED OCTOBER)*

VIBRATE: LIKE QUAKE: (THING) The ground, vibrating just like in a quake...the air vibrating too. (Unknown)

VIBRATE: LIKED PLUCKED STRING: (PERSON) His eyes stopped bugging out, but he continued to vibrate like a plucked string. (*ABANDONED IN DEATH* by J. D. Robb)

VOICE HISSED: LIKE A SNAKE: (THING) He hissed like a snake. "Ain't none of your business," he said. (*POWER PLAY* by Catherine Coulter)

VOICE TREMBLING: LIKE HER LEGS: (PERSON) As she spoke, her voice wanted to tremble like her legs, but she fought to keep it steady and light. (*THE BECOMING* by Nora Roberts)

VOICE: LIKE FLASHES OF LIGHTNING: (THING) She heard the voice more often now, sounding in her head, not a voice, really, but the words, like flashes of lightning. (*RECKONING* by Catherine Coulter)

VOICE: LIKE GALLOPING HORSES: (THING) ...her language sounded like galloping horses, a stampede that I could not arrest with my ear for even a second. *(Readers Digest TOWARD MORE PICTURESQUE SPEECH)*

VOICE: LIKE MULTIPLE KNIVES TWISTING IN WOUND: (THING) Her voice was like multiple knives, twisting in a festering wound. (Unknown)

VOICE: LIKE MUSIC: (PERSON) He was tall and straight, with dark hair waving to his shoulders and eyes as blue as Bluebells. His voice was like music in her head and set her heart to dancing. (JEWELS OF THE SUN by Nora Roberts)

VOICE: LIKE MUSIC: (THING) His voice, rising and falling like music on the words, lulled Jude into propping her elbows on the table, resting her chin on her fists. *(JEWELS OF THE SUN* by Nora Roberts*)*

VOICE: LIKE RUSTY LOCK: (THING) His voice sounded hoarse, and awkward, like a rusty lock. (*TREASURE ISLAND* by Robert Louis Stevenson)

VOICE: LIKE TAUT ROPE: (THING) The man was not only red in the face, but spoke as hoarse as a crow, and his voice shook, too, like a taut rope. (*TREASURE ISLAND* by Robert Louis Stevenson)

VOICE: LIKE VIPER: (THING) her tongue was like a viper. (*CIRCLE OF FATE* by Charlotte Lamb)

WADDLE: LIKE DUCK: (PERSON) ... waddled like a duck. (Author)

WADDLE: LIKE OVERWEIGHT WOMAN: (PERSON) ... waddled like an overweight woman. (Author)

WAIT: LIKE ETERNITY: (PERSON) ... she made a heroic effort to pin an expression of polite interest on her face and waited for what seemed like an eternity. (*LOVE UPON THE WIND* by Sally Stewart)

WALK ACROSS: LIKE SACRILEGE: LAWN: (PLACE) Walking across the thick, springy grass seemed almost like a sacrilege, but it was a sin she couldn't resist. *(JEWELS OF THE SUN by Nora Roberts)*

WALK ALL OVER: LIKE DOORMAT: (PERSON) like a doormat, she let him walk all over her. (*CIRCLE OF FATE* by Charlotte Lamb)

WALK: LIKE CELEBRITY: ROAD: (PLACE) The avenue was gilded with gold yet the leaves hadn't yet started to fall. Jenny raised her eyes to the garland above that was so stark against the cloudless sky. It was picture book perfect. Perhaps tomorrow there would be some scattered over the sidewalk, hiding some of the grey. That was truly her favorite time; she walked over them like a celebrity to her own movie premier, her head held high and her eyes higher. She sucked in the air, how she'd missed the moistness after the dry August heat. She could wear her woolen coats and boots right to her knees. She was the queen of her own life and the trees stood as if dressed for her coronation. The street lamps sent down a soft glow and the hum of the city around her was better than an orchestra. This was the start of the rest of her life, she could feel it. (Unknown)

WALK: LIKE LONG WALK ON SHORT DOCK: (PERSON) like taking a long walk on a short dock. (Weather reporter on *KUSI* 26Jan2024)

WALK: LIKE PAIR OF CONSPIRATORS: (PERSON) they walked to the door like a pair of conspirators. (Unknown)

WALK: LIKE POETS: (PERSON) The people walked like prophets and like poets, tall men with black hats and women as tall in bright colorful skirts. (*THE LIVING REED* by Pearl S. Buck)

WALK: LIKE PROPHETS: (PERSON) The people walked like prophets and like poets, tall men with black hats and women as tall in bright colorful skirts. (*THE LIVING REED* by Pearl S. Buck)

WALK: LIKE THERE'S FIRE IN BOOTS: (PERSON) marching around like there's fire in her boots. (*ABANDONED IN DEATH* by J. D. Robb)

WALK: LIKE WADING SILVER RIVER: (PERSON) She walked through the mist like a woman wading through a silver river. (*JEWELS OF THE SUN* by Nora Roberts)

WALK: LOOKED LIKE WARRIOR: (PERSON) There was purpose in her steps and determination in her demeanor. She looked like a warrior going into battle. (*QUINN* by Iris Johansen)

WAR: FELT LIKE THE APOCALYPSE: (THING) He awakened "to the sound of planes and the loud explosions of rockets - even before the dawn prayer. It felt like the apocalypse." (*INTERNET*)

WAR-LIKE: INSECT: HORNET: (THING) war-like (Unknown)

WARM AIR: LIKE SUMMER: (THING) The air seemed warmer, almost like summer despite the wind, with the fragrance of flowers that scattered through the grass and lay on the cemetery's dead suddenly wild and sweet. (*JEWELS OF THE SUN* by Nora Roberts)

WARM AIR: LIKE VELVET ON SKIN: (PERSON) She stood quietly, the warm air like velvet on her skin, the light wind stirring her hair. (*RECKONING* by Catherine Coulter)

WAVE: LIKE GROUND SWELL: ROAD: (PLACE) "[He] was silent, looking into the distance ahead, along the road, along the white road that waved gently in the heat, like a ground swell." *(THE WINTER OF OUR DISCONTENT by John Steinbeck)*

WAVE: LIKE KIDS: (PERSON) matters were jumping and waving their hands for attention like kids in school. (*THE WINTER OF OUR DISCONTENT* by John Steinbeck)

WAVER: LIKE WORLD SEEN THROUGH WATER: ATTIC: (PLACE) My attic is not a dark and spidery prison for the broken and abandoned. It has windows with small panes so old that the light comes through lavender and the outside wavers—like a world seen through water. (*THE WINTER OF OUR DISCONTENT* by John Steinbeck)

WAVY: LIKE RIVER: (THING) Her artistic vocabulary included a series of ascending rounded stone or treelike forms, a jagged lightning bolt and a flat, wavy shape like a river. (*INSIGHT* Article by Jane Addams Allen)

WEAK: LIKE FRAIL VICTORIAN LADIES: (PERSON) weakness made them act like frail Victorian ladies who have to run for the fainting couch at the first hint of conflict. (*LEAGUE OF POWER* 8Feb2024)

WEAK: LIKE HYSTERICAL WOMAN: (PERSON) He watched Kent worry the pillow fringe some more. How could he be so weak, like a hysterical woman? (*VORTEX* by Catherine Coulter)

WEAR: LIKE SECOND SKIN: (PERSON) He saw Natalie pull her shoulders back, coach her expression into one of serene control. Her Armani suit was stark black, conservative, so stylish it had turned heads of passersby when she's stepped out of her limo at the northwest gate to meet him. She wore power well, like a comfortable second skin. She added a slight, subtle smile as they walked in, a smile that said she would rule over her own reactions, and her own personal universe, come what may. She was, he decided, quite remarkable. (*POWER PLAY* by Catherine Coulter)

WEAR: LIKE TROPHY: PROGRESSIVE: (PERSON) "Progressivism will hollow out your religion and wear its skin like a trophy." (Auron MacIntyre quoted by Michael Reagan in *NEWSMAX*)

WEAVE TUNNEL: LIKE ARCHWAYS: RIVER: (PLACE) In the heart of the forest, an idle river carried all the debris that fell in from above slowly downstream. Large boughs sprouted from the trees and reached into the murky water as if trying to scoop up the swarming fish. Although the warm water was an olive color from the swirling mud and algae, you could see the underwater wildlife flourish in the shallow part. Swamp-like vegetation and old, rotting trees crept into the river's edge and created slimy pools of debris from withered leaves, twigs and lemma. Above the mass of water, high branches wove a tunnel of green leaves like archways in a church to protect from strong sunlight. (Unknown)

WHEEL: LIKE SPARROW HAWK: ATTACK: (THING) It rose suddenly upward, and with a speed incomprehensible wheeled like a sparrow hawk and dove straight .... (*TARZAN AT THE EARTH'S CORE* by Edgar Rice Burroughs)

WHIMPER: LIKE CHILD: (PERSON) He leaned out over the cliff, straddling the strong branch, and tied the thick leather thong to it. Then he took the other end of the string and tied it securely around his neck. He made several knots behind his ear, and then slowly, carefully, he crept out on the branch. The little man clung to the wood with both hands for a moment. His eyes looked directly up into the sun, and he whimpered like a child who is afraid that something is going to hurt. Then he released one hand, and the other. He dropped a few feet and, in the morning sun, swung back and forth like a lazy pendulum. The branch creaked as he swung. After a few seconds, he reached up to the leather thong and dried to grasp it and lift himself up. His mouth opened and contorted, but no sound came. The legs convulsed and drew themselves up, almost to his chest. He made one more attempt to pull himself up, then his hands fell back and settled by his side and he swung back and forth in a wide arc. He hung like a marionette on a stick and moved no more. (*THE DAY CHRIST DIED* by Jim Bishop)

WHIMPER: LIKE LAZY PENDULUM: (PERSON) He leaned out over the cliff, straddling the strong branch, and tied the thick leather thong to it. Then he took the other end of the string and tied it securely around his neck. He made several knots behind his ear, and then slowly, carefully, he crept out on the branch. The little man clung to the wood with both hands for a moment. His eyes looked directly up into the sun, and he whimpered like a child who is afraid that something is going to hurt. Then he released one hand, and the other. He dropped a few feet and, in the morning sun, swung back and forth like a lazy pendulum. The branch creaked as he swung. After a few seconds, he reached up to the leather thong and dried to grasp it and lift himself up. His mouth opened and contorted, but no sound came. The legs convulsed and drew themselves up, almost to his chest. He made one more attempt to pull himself up, then his hands fell back and settled by his side and he swung back and forth in a wide arc. He hung like a marionette on a stick and moved no more. (*THE DAY CHRIST DIED* by Jim Bishop)

WHINNY SOUND: LIKE FRIGHTENED COLT: (THING) I heard a crunching sound and a whinny like a frightened colt, and quick steps in the hall and silence. *(THE WINTER OF OUR DISCONTENT* by John Steinbeck*)*

WHIP: ACTION: DRIVE: (PERSON) Clouds wisped through them. Yes, like smoke, and the sun slanted down, winter thin. He had his first experience with switchback roads, and took it easy mostly because he wanted to see everything all at once. (*NIGHTWORK* by Nora Roberts)

WHIRLING: LIKE CLOUDS OF GNATS: (PERSON) The dim room seemed swarming with particles of brilliant light moving and whirling like clouds of gnats. I guess they were not really there but only prickles of weariness swimming in the fluid of my eyes, but they were very convincing. (*THE WINTER OF OUR DISCONTENT* by John Steinbeck)

WINCING FROM STINGING SNOW: LIKE THOUSANDS OF TINY NEEDLES: (THING) Wincing as his bare face was stung by wind-driven snow like thousands of tiny cold needles. (Unknown)

WIND BLOWS DUST: LIKE SLUGGISH SMOKE: (THING) A gentle wind followed the rain clouds, driving them on northward, a wind that softly clashed the drying corn. A day went by and the wind increased, steady, unbroken by gusts. The dust from the roads fluffed up and spread out and fell on the weeds beside the fields, and fell into the fields a little way. Now the wind grew strong and hard and it worked at the rain crust in the corn fields. Little by little the sky was darkened by the mixing dust, and the wind felt over the earth, loosened by the dust, and carried it away. The wind grew stronger. The rain crust broke and the dust lifted up out of the fields and drove gray plumes into the air like sluggish smoke. The corn threshed the wind and made a dry, rushing sound. The finest dust did not settle back to earth now, but disappeared into the darkening sky. (*THE GRAPES OF WRATH* by John Steinbeck)

WIND DROVE MIST: LIKE SHEEP: (THING) An eager wind sprang from nowhere and drove the mist like sheep. (*THE WINTER OF OUR DISCONTENT* by John Steinbeck)

WIND EXPERIENCE: LIKE STICKING HEAD OUT CAR WINDOW: (THING) The experience is a little like sticking your head out a car window at highway speed. The wind blows so hard you forget to breathe. *(SUCCESS November 1987)*

WIND OVER HILL: LIKE DISCARDED BELT: STREET:(PLACE) The street wound over the hill like a carelessly discarded belt, grey and cracked with age. On each side the houses are separated by yards large enough to accommodate farm animals, but this is no rural district. The homes are many times larger than even the biggest of families might need, yet in each are mostly parents with one child. To each dwelling there are more sports cars than people and kitchens that cost more than our homes just a block over. But I can ride my bike down here, enjoying the wide avenues, the leafy green trees and the relative safety now that the security guards patrol. There is talk of the residents paying to have the road repaved; they don't want the same repair service as the rest of us, nor the same schools or health service. Our parents are the nurses, the technicians and the fast food servers and they would like us to stay in our ramshackle boxes and never enter their plush neighborhoods. (Unknown)

WIND SOUND: LIKE WOMAN WEEPING: (THING) The wind came up strong and sounded like a woman weeping. *(JEWELS OF THE SUN* by Nora Roberts)

WINDY: LIKE WIND TUNNELS: ROOMS: (PLACE) There was no central heat in the house. In winter the rooms were like wind tunnels and the air smelled damp. *(CIRCLE OF FATE* by Charlotte Lamb)

WINE GLASS REVOLVED: LIKE PROPELLER: I remember white wine. The brittle glass revolved like a propeller. *(THE WINTER OF OUR DISCONTENT* by John Steinbeck)

WOODLAND: LIKE DROPLET OF PARADISE: FOREST: (PLACE) The woodland is like a droplet of paradise. The air is still, only the laughter of children in a nearby park reminds me that I'm still in the city. Here my dog can run free for hours and I can stop to watch nature. The sunlight streams in like it is more pure than the light I feel downtown, white, yet liquid gold at the same time. Nearby, on a rotting spindly tree, is a woodpecker hunting for insects, its brilliant red crest rocking back and forth as it pecks. Tiny chunks of wood fall to the leaf litter below, the sound dissipating into the woodland around. (Unknown)

WORD SOUND: LIKE BLOWTORCH: (THING) the sound of a word edged with blue flame like a blowtorch. *(THE WINTER OF OUR DISCONTENT* by John Steinbeck*)*

WORDS FIXED: LIKE A ROCK: (THING) his words were like a rock firmly fixed in a world of shifting ideological tides. (KOINIONA HOUSE article by Ron Matsen)

WORDS PIERCED CONSCIOUSNESS: LIKE TINY POISONED DARTS: (THING) his words pierced her consciousness like so many tiny poisoned darts. (*HEARTLAND* by Bethany Campbell)

WORDS REPEATED: LIKE LITANY: (THING) ... repeated the words to himself over and over again, like a litany. (*THE GUNS OF NAVORONE* by Alistair Maclean)

WORDS RESOUNDED: LIKE CRACK OF RIFLE: (THING) The hasty words resounded like the crack of a rifle, shattering the peace, splintering in the still sweet air like jagged missiles. (*COUNTRY OF THE HEART* by Robyn Donald)

WORE BLUE JEANS AND DENIM JACKET: LIKE OTHERS: (PERSON) A tall man stood in the doorway. He held a crushed Stetson hat under his arm while he combed his long, black, damp hair straight back. Like the others he wore blue jeans and a short denim jacket. When he had finished combing his hair, he moved into the room, and he moved with a majesty only achieved by royalty and master craftsmen. He was a jerkline skinner, the prince of the ranch, capable of driving ten, sixteen, even twenty mules with a single line to the leaders. He was capable of killing a fly on the wheeler's butt with a bull whip without touching the mule. There was a gravity in his manner and a quiet so profound that all talk stopped when he spoke. His authority was so great that his word was taken on any subject, be it politics or love. This was Slim, the jerkline skinner. His hatchet face was ageless. He might have been thirty-five or fifty. His ear heard more than was said to him, and his slow speech had overtones not of thought, but of understanding beyond thought. His hands, large and lean, were as delicate in their actions as those of a temple dancer. (*OF MICE AND MEN* by John Steinbeck)

WORE BOOTS: LIKE BOSS: (PERSON) At that moment a young man came into the bunk-house; a thin young man with a brown face, with brown eyes and a head of tightly curled hair. He wore a work glove on his left hand, and, like the boss, he wore high-heeled boots. (*OF MICE AND MEN* by John Steinbeck)

WORK: LIKE AUTOMATIONS: (PERSON) they worked like two automations programmed to ignore each other. (*HEARTLAND* by Bethany Campbell)

WORK: LIKE HORSE: (PERSON) He worked like a horse all the school season and felt if he was required to do more, he'd be only skin and bone. (*THE RADIO BOYS AT MOUNTAIN PASS* by Allen Chapman)

WRAPPED: LIKE MUMMY: (PERSON) He swung his legs off the bed, absently noting that they were still wrapped, mummy-like, in the covers. (*FEAR THE DARK* by Kay Hooper)

WRITE: LIKE QUOTE MACHINE: (PERSON) He was a like a quote machine—feed him anything and he'll write an op-ed. (Unknown)

<back>

SUMMARY

Metaphors give color to our words.

    I started out studying the creations of authors I enjoyed reading. I sought out other good writers. Then I associated with many other book readers to hear what books they found good reads. The common link between all of these was the visual images that the best writers created in the minds of readers who eagerly devoured the words that they found. Comments like, "I couldn't put it down!" gave me a great clue that a particular author was likely very descriptive in telling their story. It turns out that these authors sold the most books and made the most income. Among the factors that make a book "a keeper" are content and descriptions of the people, places, and things that are sown together to make the book a top seller.

<back>

ABOUT ROBERT BRENNER

He began researching descriptive language 15 years ago when he made a commitment to improve his writing style. He collected all the words, phrases, and expressions he could find in an earnest effort to make writing come alive for himself and for other writers. He identified and studied the most successful authors, and then he created tools to help other authors achieve writing that amazes even them.

Robert Brenner is an engineer, consultant, college professor, and teacher with extensive experience in research and information publishing.

A retired Navy mustang (enlisted then officer) with 11 submarine deployments under his belt, he holds a bachelor's degree in electrical engineering (BSEE) from the University of New Mexico, a master's degree in electrical engineering (MSEE) from the Naval Postgraduate School, and a master's degree in systems management (MSEE) from the University of Southern California.

He was designated a Very High Speed Integrated Circuit (VHSIC) microelectronics pioneer by the DOD and served in defense R&D before dedicating his energies to researching and writing books full time.

He has been a guest speaker at national conferences and symposiums and is the author of over 60 books including *Descriptive Language for Writers and Speakers*, *The Descriptive Expressions of Nora Roberts*, *Power Up! The Smart Guide to Home Solar Power*, *Going Solar: A Homeowner's Experience,*; *Solar Case Study: 5.0 kW Home Power Generator*, *Supernatural & Strange Happenings in the Bible*, *Bartering Basics* and *Bigfoot Encounters in Michigan's Thumb*. He also wrote over 275 articles on business and computer applications. He taught at the high school, community college, university, and graduate school levels. A futurist, he enjoys the challenge of research and is currently sharing his knowledge with professionals and home owners worldwide.

The author can be reached by email at brennerbooks@san.rr.com
<back>

OTHER BOOKS BY ROBERT C. BRENNER

Bartering Basics: How to Trade for Food, Products, and Services
   Bigfoot Encounters in Michigan's Thumb
   Descriptive Language for Writers and Speakers
   Michigan Bigfoot Encounters (Upper Peninsula)
   Pricing Tables - (9 national regions, multiple editions)
   Pricing Tactics
   Pricing Web Services
   Power Up! The Smart Guide to Home Solar Power
   Small Business Guide to Pricing
   Solar Case Study: 5.0 kW Home Power Generator
   Solar Case Study: 6.4 kW Home Power Generator
   Solar Case Study: 7.4 kW Home Power Generator
   Solar Power: How to Construct (and Use) the 45W Harbor Freight Solar Kit
   Special Report: Scoping Services
   Special Report: Software Services
   Special Report: Virtual Service Earnings
   Special Report: Virtual Services
   Supernatural and Strange Happenings in the Bible
   Supernatural and Strange Happenings in the Family
   Survive a Power Outage: Emergency Lighting
   The Descriptive Expressions of Nora Roberts
   Writer's Guide to Descriptive Language

COMING BOOKS

The Descriptive Expressions of John Steinbeck
The Descriptive Expressions of Catherine Coulter
The Descriptive Expressions of Tom Clancy

<back>

Thank you for reading this book. If you enjoyed it, please take a moment to leave a review at your favorite retailer or library.

www.ingramcontent.com/pod-product-compliance
Lightning Source LLC
Chambersburg PA
CBHW020804160426
43192CB00006B/433